T0116483

The Need and Application of
PRACTICAL HOLINESS
Divine Cooperation

GERALD S MELTON

authorHOUSE®

AuthorHouse™
1663 Liberty Drive
Bloomington, IN 47403
www.authorhouse.com
Phone: 833-262-8899

Published by AuthorHouse 04/06/2023

ISBN: 979-8-8230-0557-9 (sc)
ISBN: 979-8-8230-0556-2 (e)

Contents

Introduction

Have you ever been overwhelmed by sinful struggles? Perhaps a struggle to say no to alcohol. You do not want to, but struggle and cannot seem to cut off the temptation at its root? Perhaps lust has kept you at bay and will not let you sail out to sea to venture into the Lords plans for your life?

These are common struggles we all seem to go through from time to time. We can gain strength through cooperation with God (practical holiness) to overcome in our life. Practical holiness can help us with the spiritual challenges and common struggles with sin.

The Need and Application of Practical Holiness

THERE IS A CHALLENGE TO PRACTICAL HOLINESS

The Spiritual Leader faces many challenges and temptations today. For example, a Bi-vocational pastor faces workplace animosity, peer pressure, contentions, etc. The local Church pastor faces community opposition, lack of support, temptations of all kinds, and lack of time for well-planned godly action. The Christian on the job goes through mental challenges and sometimes violence to walk Christlike. Because of the many challenges that the Spiritual Leader faces, practical holiness must be thought out and applied as second nature by them.

Whatever your ministry, calling, or vocation; I want this book to accommodate you on your journey to cooperate with God in holy living.

Follow peace with all men, and holiness, without which no man shall see the Lord: Hebrews 12:14 (KJV)

Therefore, the necessity and need for a book to help us to cooperate with God in our part which is yielding to him in his sovereign leadership over us.

THE NEED FOR PRACTICAL HOLINESS

Holiness is essential for many reasons. First, it is important because God demands it. Second, to succeed, we must live out practical holiness, so we live in God's approval and blessing in our lives.

We must realize that without holiness, no man will see God. The conclusion is that those who are unholy will be judged. Now, just what are holiness and ungodliness? The best way I can describe it is that holiness is to live under the lordship of Jesus Christ, while ungodliness is to forsake the lordship of Jesus Christ over us. This definition means we can walk in holiness all our lives by staying near to the Holy Spirit. We know better as followers of Jesus Christ to remain near to the presence of God more than unbelievers would. It is blatant wrong to walk forgetful of God and his nearness to us. If we do not occupy within the framework of God's great will for us, there we compromise the integrity of every place in our lives before him. God's judgment will eventually come upon the one who refuses to reform and conform to God's lordship; simply because they would not heed God's Word and ways.

Holiness has the idea of being set apart for God and being in his service. To be this kind of vessel, we must be found faithful. If we are not dependable over this service, whatever kind it is, we will lose our stewardship of it. The person must be dedicated to God's cause and exercise fidelity to him. They must perform their purpose or reason for being unto God specifically. Just as a person learns their new job at a place of employment and faithfully does their part every day, so the faithful steward must exercise their duty and service to God in holiness. We all live in a probationary period until God calls us out of it, and my point is that we must fulfill our responsibilities to him all in a way pleasing to him to be found faithful. Faithfulness will mean we will continue serving God in eternity in the new appointed stewardship of his choosing. Whenever an opportunity arises to use our stewardship for God, then we need a fiery and zealous spirit to receive and act on those opportunities. To act upon those opportunities means we utilize our talents, gifts, and abilities to work on and accomplish God's will and avoid sloth. Our mission can only be achieved through walking with God, knowing and exercising our gifts, and blessing other people in some new or fresh way.

Another reason we need practical holiness is so we can overcome temptation and sin's power. We know evil exists because there is a devil and a kingdom called "the gates of hell," from which these things operate and come to us. Satan continues to plan our demise. As we apply practical holiness, we set ourselves up to fellowship and commune with God and identify with his cause. We then find it easy to do his work in life. His presence will give us divine favor if we daily stay acquainted with him. This divine favor is how we learn to bring heaven to wherever we go. God, through our union, will give us Jesus Christ's victory over evil. Evil is a state of living without God, and we can reckon sin negated by Christ's work at Calvary.

Practical holiness helps us to live out God's will because we set ourselves apart for his service and are called to be separate from the evil of this age. We will be engaged in the work of God. Living out his will is the thing that matters. We can serve God by learning and obeying his will; then, as we live out that will at every opportunity and wholeheartedly obey God in all of life, we will be a chosen vessel. Yielding to God's will in this way is supposed to be what our walk and worship are about.

If we practice holiness, we must conform to Jesus Christ. Conforming means presenting ourselves to God through Jesus, and the idea of following him comes to play. Conforming to Jesus means becoming more like him, as he did the Father's will perfectly. Therefore, we strive to do the Father's will and work at getting better and better at it. The growth of this kind will take God working through us.

It becomes our goal to accomplish God's will throughout our earthly sojourn. We follow God's direction and will in all our growth and change phases of life. If we live this way, our eternal reflection of Jesus Christ will glorify God and shine brightly. By heeding God's Word, disciplining ourselves to dialogue with God in spiritual disciplines, and conforming to Jesus Christ through discipleship, this will become a reality.

Another aspect of practical holiness is being usable and available for God's service. If we cannot or will not be functional or available for God, how can he ever use us for his work and purpose? This availability is a defining principle for any ministry a person might have for God. Knowing God's purpose and using it to do God's bidding is critical for ministry success. In all situations, we must apply ourselves in purpose and application to the honor of God, doing this among the community of saints and unbelievers. We need to pray God would supply any lack that would hinder God's business and progress. We must be usable if we will be God's holy vessels who promote and enforce his order in life.

One important reason to live out practical holiness is to keep an ongoing witness of God: both what he has done for us and who he is to us. If we lose our holiness walk, then we jeopardize our whole testimony before other people. Our testimony demonstrates how God is a witness of himself among the doubters and unbelievers. These are testimonies that anytime people can inquire of God, repent, believe in Jesus Christ, and be given eternal life. Our testimony needs to stand in any community we are a part of. The drive of this ongoing testimony is for us to completely fulfill what God has called us to do and be. The point of our testimony should show who Jesus is, what he did, what that means, and the danger of rejecting him.

Practical holiness is needed so we will effectively do God's bidding. We must be about his business by conducting his purpose for our life. God has called each of us to a purpose. Each believer has an office to fill. Everything we do has a time limit, so we must act now before God. It behooves us to learn to follow the Spirit and express Jesus Christ at the place when testimony is needed. We can do God's bidding through being living vessels in his service; this is achieved by offering ourselves to him as living sacrifices.

Practical holiness brings with it the idea of being of valuable service to God and his people. We are not doing a whole lot if we render no service to God or any other people in a loving and godly way. Our service should be the kind that equips God's people, edifies them, and builds them up for his glory. We render valuable service to God when we consistently offer ourselves to God's use and be faithful in it. Such reliable service occurs as we take advantage of the opportunity that presents itself. Where is the need which continues to arise for our service; that is where we need to be? We need to serve others as unto the Lord. So, we need a willing attitude, and we should be available and stay qualified for the master's use.

The need to be set apart is part of our need for practical holiness. We cannot serve two masters. Either we loved one or the other. God demands we be set apart unto him and for his good pleasure. Each person entering some service for God must know spiritual disciplines that allow a person to enter and stay in God's presence. When we are saturated in God's presence, we find favor, and God can work through us. As we continue daily seeking this condition of usableness, God favors our participation. By spending this time with God, we learn his leading and make ourselves available.

The need for practical holiness is a need to continue in ones calling. Practical holiness is to be set apart for God's service; this means that we continue to exercise our calling. It must be our attitude and motive to please God with joy in any service we give him. The goal of our call and service is to be about God's business. We must stay conformed to God's will if we will be about his work. Prayer is the key to aligning our call with God's will. Conformity demands that we daily bear our cross. We can only accept that cross with God's help. Our goal is always to have a living testimony in word and deed unto the true God and who he is and what he has done. If we have such a testimony, we must be in communion and fellowship with him. Our goal is to continue to grow in him.

Our goal in practical holiness is to be busy in service to God. This type of service is summed up in a word called "occupy." This word means to be here waiting for Jesus Christ's return and staying in continuous service doing his will unto the day God calls us home. If we achieve this kind of service, we need to seek, know, and always obey God's directive will for our lives. This service is an ongoing process where we continually apply ourselves to God's will and work. We are encouraged in this kind of process until we give our account to God. Each day is our opportunity to serve God vigorously. We take advantage of this in every place people assemble as a community. We are engaged in exchanging how we apply ourselves now unto Jesus Christ, his cause, work, will, etc., for eternal stewardship if we are faithful. We desire an excellent account to give to God on accountability day. The way this is achieved is for us, in this earthly probation, to labor for God's cause until we enter our eternity.

If we have something worth living,

keeping, and giving, we must walk in the victory Jesus Christ has given us from our initial born-again experience forward. Victory is not going around winning against people every time we have a personality struggle. It is, though, a victory of starting our day with God and ending it with him without loss of divine approval. Only as we serve God in his presence will we be assured of the victory. We must learn to be the vessel God chooses to operate through that brings success. We are to submit ourselves to God's authority anytime he calls. We can count on God giving us a Word for the people and even at specific times when people are going through things. We, also, will receive God's exceptional help to face off and win against evil forces. Staying available and ready for God is our choice. Being prepared requires intentionality and being available and giving ourselves to attending to God as we are able.

If we accept practical holiness, then we must strive for perfection.

Having therefore these promises, dearly beloved, let us cleanse ourselves

from all filthiness of the flesh and spirit, perfecting holiness in the fear of God.
2 Corinthians 7:1 (KJV)

This perfection is not sinlessness. However, in Jesus Christ, we should find we do not have to sin every day. But this perfection is continual growth and relationship with God. It is God's will we conform to Jesus Christ and his divine plan. We will have to stay in God's will to do so because we cannot continue apart from him. So, we use spiritual disciplines to draw close to him with the expectation of daily impartations of God's presence and instructions, so he enables us to do his will by his indwelling presence. As we perceive God's will, we should immediately obey. The Holy Spirit will inspire and guide us. Let us keep in mind that Satan seeks to break our fragile bond of a loving relationship between God and us so that he can interject discouragement. The little foxes spoil the vines. We must guard our labor, our deposit in the gospel, and the remarkable life of Jesus within our hearts. How is all this done? This kind of life occurs through a vibrant relationship with Jesus, from the born-again experience to a long-term relationship.

THE APPLICATION OF PRACTICAL HOLINESS

As Leaders, especially preachers, we must face many temptations, trials, tests, and obstacles to accomplish what God calls us to do. The last thing we want to happen is to shipwreck our ministry because we failed to observe the applications of practical holiness.

We must learn that our ministries suffer shipwreck if our personal lives gets out of order. So, each of us must develop our own system to keep our life up to date. This plan to update our life is our first step in applying practical holiness. I say each of us must do this because not one of us is the same. So, we all must learn to respond to God's leading in a way we apply it to our life first. But how do we do this? I use what I call Phio (Put your house in order) system. My simple system includes:

1. Review my testimony.
2. Review my bible study technique.
3. Staying ready for speaking events.

4. Do a thinking update to get my mind out of routine and to think freely and systematically.
5. Do or go over my budget.
6. Review and grow in my purpose.
7. Review how discipleship training is going by using a system of application.
8. Make a spiritual warfare plan page and put it to use every other week.
9. Go over your goals and see where you are at, and you are getting things done.
10. Make a pleasant attitude sheet for future ruff times to remind you of godly motives and intentions.
11. Write out one's prayer list, times, and goals. How is it going?
12. What is one's spiritual life maintenance sheet, so if you get ruffed up in spiritual warfare, you can return to what is important to you?
13. How is your preparation for preaching?

Our goal in all this is to be fully prepared and ready to live out our response to holiness by staying in step with the Holy Spirit. Our goal is not to make ourselves more holy because that is God's work but to respond affirmatively to the work of his hand during the challenges to our practical holiness responses. If we continue to put our life before God for his purposes, then he will allow many opportunities to come our way so that we will have the possibility to be successful. Wherever we find ourselves is an excellent place to practice obedience to God and his Word. Practical holiness is a continuous response to arising needs that persons and communities may have to draw closer to Jesus. We cannot help facilitating if we do not have our life in order and obedience to God. Therefore, we recognize practical holiness demands we get our lives in order according to God's will.

In the application of holiness, going right along the lines of where we are spiritually is knowing where other people are at spiritually. If we are preachers and pastors serving God and preaching his Word, and we cannot see where people are at in their spiritual walk and life, then how can we lead them where God wants to take them? Further, if we do not know where they are, how can we ever know where God wants them to go? Preachers are not travel agents, but they are more like tour guides who walk with the congregation members, bringing them where God wants them to go in life's journey. A great indicator of where a person or group is at is by the behavior they exhibit. What do they do, both during worship and bible study and when they are not spiritual? What motives drive their work and life? Secretly evaluate the spirit behind it and see what's behind it. What people do and what they cherish describes who or what is central to them. As we notice their heart's desires, we can see what we should pray for on their behalf to God. This concern and opportunity are our time to do our preparations and go to bat for them. So, it is in daily life we learn the terrible struggles our people engage in, and we take them to God in our prayer closet. We must promptly intercede and deal with the genuine issues they face or stand losing them. If we will not fight for them, why should God let us pastor them? We will have to prepare, pray, and get a Word from God for them. We may have to confront them.

The application of practical holiness also means we control the atmosphere of our communities by directing the spirituality of the community. Now, how exactly is this done? First, we must establish and affirm that God has asked us to be spiritual leaders. Our leadership is always being challenged and must constantly be re-affirmed. Satan would love to remove religious order and establish anarchy or non-godly order or chaos. Our job is to enforce God's order by his authority. We must prepare by watching, regulating, praying, and interposing within the community atmosphere enforcing the Christ-like ideals. It is the communities' responsibility to keep the divine order in motion. It is the spiritual director's job to watch (see) what is going on and take the initiative to step in when the need arises. In our tasks and duties, we must follow God's direction and keep ourselves available to him. The reason we do this is to guide the atmosphere back to God's plan should it get sidetracked or corrupted. It is the privilege of the spiritual leaders to know and understand godly policy, godly procedures, prayer, and concern over this. We must set the truth in motion through love. This policy is especially true in the Church community.

The application of practical holiness also means that our lives should be examples of a blessed godly life. God calls us all to experience the blessed life as we hold to Jesus in godliness. Again, if we waste away God's intentions and blessings, that may cut off his blessings for a while. Do not treat the blessed life with contempt because it is from God. If we follow Jesus by hearing his command to believe, love, and obey him, we will experience his faithfulness. As we allow the Holy Spirit to fulfill God's will through us, we experience life and life more abundantly. We must begin the process of taking steps now to abide in Jesus Christ continually. This kind of walk is learned. Jesus offers us a bright future, a fulfilling life now, and liberation from our past. All this freedom is, so we go on living to please God by bearing godly fruit which lasts. Jesus told us that if we remain in him and he remains in us, we will bear fruit which remains; Jesus and the Father will come to us, and we can ask anything, and God will do it.

The application of practical holiness requires a working definition. My definition is: practical holiness responds in obedience to God by our choices, actions, behavior, lifestyle, motives, and attitudes; with the Holy Spirit's help. Every believer must commit to God through holiness. I am not talking about self-righteousness or in-ordinate self-perfection but doing all we can to walk in unbroken fellowship with God. In holiness, we are all called to serve God and one another. We are set apart for God's purposes, and we cooperate in every way we can or are called by him to do so. We cooperate with God, so always, our light remains shining in Jesus Christ. At every choice, before us, we sow into the Spirit of God and follow his will, so godly character is established. We cooperate with the Holy Spirit in our spiritual sanctification and growth because our identity through Jesus is adopted children of God. Who we are demands we live following God's leading. The only way to learn this is by following the Holy Spirit in complying with God's Word.

Is the application of practical holiness possible? I believe we Christians have a model and person to follow in Jesus Christ and a host of other Christ-like people. Every spiritual Christian leader in faith is a demonstration of a Christ-like life. They model what it is like to follow Jesus. We must be like Jesus Christ, who pleased the Father through the Holy Spirit and had a good report to give. Every opportunity is our chance to follow God's leading and to do his will. Wherever we find ourselves, we can cooperate with God to do what he requests. We can communicate Jesus Christ to the communities we are a part of. If we grow in this way, we will be pleasing God, making us more like Jesus. So, how can this be or be done? Well, there are numerous approaches to obedience: let us start with just obeying and following God's instructions. Next, in our devotion time, we utilize spiritual formation to enter God's presence to acquire divine favor, instructions, and approval. Then, listening, character, and follow-through are essential elements to living out the answers God gives.

There is a victory in the application of

practical holiness which God gives those who cooperate with him. As we learn to cut off that which is not helpful to following Jesus, we gain victory to do God's will. We can cut off many sins and their source by acknowledging the Spirit and his work. Also, as we apply Jesus Christ's finished work of Calvary to the bite and power of sin, we walk the victory. As we continue in Jesus, the power of evil begins to lose its hold over our lives. Whenever sin attempts a root in our lives, the victory comes from the Lord and our cooperation with him. Our job is to yield to the Spirit to gain victory and produce Christ-like lives because from our heart proceeds: evil communication, behavior, motives, and desires. Let us apply Calvary's love to all uprising evil so that we can walk in the victory.

The application of practical holiness requires that we learn what we can do or are to do. As we continue in life, we each find that we have options in dealing with temptations and decisions. Do we honor God or Satan (and ourselves)? Ultimately learning how to submit to Jesus Christ's Lordship is the best policy. We need to learn to direct ourselves to take the steps for and to God. All we do should lead to continued fellowship instead of independence from God. We should know the timing of when to lead in preventive and remedial situations. We must step up to the plate to gain victory during any contention from evil. We do this to glorify God and honor him in all we do individually and as a community. We continue to press on exploring and living out the will of God. As we live out our godly options and practice them, God will give us victory.

In the application of practical holiness, we will find that there are various applications required of our lives at various stages of development. First, we each must learn that God has much help to give us. We are maturing in each step and learning how to apply ourselves at those times. Second, we must become aware of all the tools that are before us today. No matter what level we are at, we can get something in training. It is our pleasure to work out that aspect for our benefit. Third, we must put the time and effort to get spiritually prepared. Our preparations prepare us for anything we will face. When we train, every time evil and godlessness raise its head; we know what to do. We prepare so we can live the continuous godly testimony, walk, and victory in Jesus. We are to prepare ourselves to respond in godliness.

If we apply practical holiness, then we must learn to cooperate daily with God. There is no place, in this life, where we have arrived. We are called to let God live through us and serve him, and to live holy and co-labor with him. This godliness requires a lifetime of submission to Jesus Christ's lordship. As we prepare ourselves, we let God have something to work within us. When we prepare, we move forward, and God will accomplish his will through us. As God does his will through us, we produce fruit that pleases him. This important fruit-bearing aspect of our lives requires God's favor and blessing. It does not happen except through struggles, trials, and pain. Satan is not going to sit and allow the fruit to ripen on our tree. He will shake it off if he can. But as we spend time before God, his blessing will manifest.

The application of practical holiness

requires our effort to resist Satan and fight off sin and temptation. Sin has dimensions to it, so we must work in Jesus's righteousness to be fit to ward it off. As we follow Jesus and the Holy Spirit, we gain the ability to say no to temptation. Sin and temptation are Satan's attempt to get us to put God out of our lives; if sin is allowed to fester, we have a much harder time fighting and resisting it. We must deal with it way before the time temptation arises. Do not let sin establish a stronghold in you. Satan will attempt to bring in divisive sin through our old nature in deeds, lifestyles, thoughts, and habits. He will try any time or place to set up shop against us. We must give Satan a fight he will never forget. Please do not make a place for him. He is seeking to create in you a life devoid of God. He wants to displace God in your life. He aims to get you to use freedom and free will contrary to cooperation with God so that he can sneer at God and say, "I'll do it my way." His pride is the worst kind because he desires a universe without God and desires to be God.

GENERAL PRACTICE OF PRACTICAL HOLINESS

Why the believer needs holiness

What does it look like for a believer to serve God in practical holiness? What does practical holiness look like in a believer's life? We understand basic facts about practical holiness. First, a spiritual leader faces attacks from the adversary known as Satan, as noted in the biblical scriptures. Secondly, we must learn to guard our words and conduct to keep our testimony. Third, sin awaits to snare the unprotected believer. And lastly, the believer must deal with sin way before the day he meets it. In our very remote communities, we see that growing in various areas within and without the need for individual persons to operate in holiness within their strict and rough community atmosphere.

Because the community abandons traditional values, there is a great need for individuals to live out practical holiness. Our nation has drifted extremely far from its moorings. Because of such settings, it has become increasingly more challenging for one to follow their belief in holiness. The bible tells us that in the last day's wickedness shall increase. We must overcome evil with good. If we do not stay up with the times, we will fall behind; this is just as real spiritually as secular. We must enter the struggle to keep our ideology of Jesus Christ's lordship, which begins at the born-again experience. We must pray that God will help us live out practical holiness. Also, we should be available to hear and apply God's Word. We want to get to the place where we serve God and other people with purpose and love. Therefore, we must pray to our God, live a new Spirit-anointed life before God unto others. We must love them into God's good plan for them. We must model the ideal life in Jesus for others.

How can we manage enemy attacks?

As we cooperate with God, we first learn that our enemy attacks us in practical holiness. Satan shows up to attack us, co-laborers of his activate, Christians become misguided, and people enter error. Knowing this happens, we realize right away that assurance, confidence, security, and understanding fall to the ground. These attacks by the enemy are a sure sign that the gates of hell are pressing. We need our armor, accept our cross, know the fundamental truths, and seek God.

> I laid me down and slept; I awaked; for the LORD sustained me. I will not be afraid of ten thousands of people, that have set themselves against me round about. Psalm 3:5-6 (KJV)

> Trust in the LORD with all thine heart; and lean not unto thine own understanding. In all thy ways acknowledge him, and he shall direct thy paths. Proverbs 3:5-6 (KJV)

We must at such times apply governing truths: what spiritual resources are available to us that instruct us in God's Word? We may have to go back to the last point where the Holy Spirit led us to gain our position as before. Where were we headed? We can use the fundamental truths to fight Satan off.

We need to recall any spiritual training and attend to our meditation to put godliness in our hearts for the Holy Spirit to use. We must identify the area we left the path and get back on and move forward. We must let God guide us since Jesus is the key to our example and experience. We may have to go to pastoral authorities. We must speak faith or scripture to ourselves. We can talk with God as well. Let us learn to position ourselves in God's presence so we can acquire divine favor for all we need. Sometimes we may need to shout the Lord's rebuke at Satan to drive him off. We can get to a good place alone and speak the truth inwardly. We must acknowledge God as we take a stand.

We may have to tell apposing spiritual opposition that we will stand against it, where God has placed us. Usually, we should pick our battles carefully and avoid violating others. But there are times we must upset people. When we talk to God, tell him what is going on and what we are going through. Let us utilize our relationship with God without bickering and complaining or fretting and fuming. Ask God for his advice and the power to do it. Let us ask, "What's going on, God?" How can I do your will in this? We must examine what is going on.

What did Satan do to start the chaos? What trigger event did we give an adverse reaction to? Let us apply truth responsibly to it and respond the right way. We must demonstrate the correct type of response which will heal the group or people involved. We must talk to contentious members to implement peaceful solutions. Another key to help us is to speak the truth in a caring way. Yes, speak God's Word to the situation in love, "Peace be still!" If we talk to a group of obnoxious people to calm them down, say something like, "What I believe would be helpful for our group is to love one another. Can we exercise love toward each other?" We must address Satan with "The Lord rebuke thee Satan." We need to manage ourselves and others with patients. Repeat to God that we need him and appreciate him and will do as he says with his help. We must speak health, maintain our life, and be responsible with our freedom before God.

We must guard our words and conduct.

We must watch and analyze the atmosphere constantly if we are leaders in a community. We will find that we are in the spotlight and observed all the time for our behavior. Either people watch for motivation or to find fault with us. Our words, tongue, character, behavior, etc., all are on the line. Our conscience is always under scrutiny and question. If we slip, lie, or do what we should not, then we may be in trouble. We must guard our conscience and maintain our walk with God, so we do not get embarrassed. If someone should find fault, immediately ask God's help right away and keep the character on course.

God *is* our refuge and strength, a very present help in trouble. Therefore, will not we fear, though the earth be removed, and though the mountains be carried into the midst of the sea; Though the waters thereof roar *and* be troubled, *though* the mountains shake with the swelling thereof. Selah. Psalm 46:1-3 (KJV)

Yea, and all that will live godly in Christ Jesus shall suffer persecution. But evil men and seducers shall wax worse and worse, deceiving, and being deceived. But continue thou in the things which thou hast learned and hast been assured of, knowing of whom thou hast learned *them*; And that from a child thou hast known the holy scriptures, which can make thee wise unto salvation through faith which is in Christ Jesus. All scripture *is* given by inspiration of God, and *is* profitable for doctrine, for reproof, for correction, for instruction in righteousness: That the man of God may be perfect, thoroughly furnished unto all good works. 2 Timothy 3:12-17 (KJV)

What hope or instruction can I offer you for times when the heat is on? We can daily program our conscience through reading and studying scripture, and we can expect God's help with our conduct and the pressures of life as we pray to him every day. The bible tells us:

> Be not deceived: evil communications corrupt good manners. 1 Corinthians 15:33 (KJV)

When this happens, we can be sure that it is not God setting us up. Satan is seeking to discourage us or give a blow to us. But if we have spent our time with God, then we can be assured that he will come through and smash Satan's plans. Now, if we are doing wrong, God will use this to humble us. The bible gives us explicit knowledge that what is unseen is more real than what is seen. There is plenty of warning in scripture to let us know that we live our lives in front of many audiences whether we realize it or not. We are before God and his hosts, Satan's hosts, the hosts of humankind, and our friends. Who we pursue, who we worship, who we love, how much time we spend working, what we do for fun, etc., all demonstrate where our hearts are? Where is God in all we do? Do we go out of our way to obey his commandments in the process, like, loving God and our neighbors? If we are going to be in the spotlight, make sure we know who we are in Jesus and where we are in him at any given moment. Satan can throw a fiery dart at us through our friends and loved ones. Without a doubt, let us have our armor ready. We can walk forward out of the encroachment of Satan before the presence of our people. When we are under pressure and the guns begin to fire, assess what is going on and take the weapons the Lord provides for you for that moment and use them. Exercise care to be proper with God, authority, and whomever you can; not all people will let you be their friend.

It is at such times we had better be able to have a solid inner dialogue. Let's keep focused and stay in context within the setting everything is happening. Avoid tripping or slipping from the sober-minded place and keep close to God through it. We must decide whether we can go on or do we need to address something first. Whisper within yourself or get to a private place where you speak the truth to the situation.

Let's square ourselves up and, with courage and confidence, face our contenders. We may apologize if we messed up or express where we are going in the dialogue. Let's not point the finger at anyone but keep our place spiritually and ask God's competency on you. Get God involved by pointing out God's leading in the situation, and remember the holy scriptures are the authoritative rule.

Keeping our focus and contextual place while being truthful to ourselves helps while we set our thinking aright. Was there an actual incident? If so, what happened? What caused this incident? What adverse reaction had occurred? What should have happened? What truth must be applied to get the proper response? In every matter that we participate in, I will point out that working to spot the truth and using it is the key to resolving our response issues. Jesus said that if we know his doctrine, then we shall know the truth, and the truth would make us free. Put everything in focus according to God's way and will using scripture, and you will be free from situational pits.

When we are in the spotlight, and our

character is in question by rogue contenders. Speak the right solutions. A good healthy word carefully spoken is in order. Address the community with truth in the open. We must speak love with firmness at this time. Rebuke without demoralizing anyone. Love and dialogue within yourself, also, with kind words.

We must make ourselves think right and speak right. We cannot allow outside forces to control us. As a man thinks, so is he. Use your adulthood and freedom responsibly. The power you have you must use wisely. As always, get God involved. Ask him to bless the situation and people. Think the right way, and do not be a victim.

We need to realize that sin waits to snare us.

When sin crouches like a snake and makes ready to bite, that is when we find out how effective our devotional time with God has been. If we had been practicing holiness up to when the enemy attacked, then we would have been well prepared for the bite of sin, just like in the days of Moses when God's children complained and were bitten by snakes. Moses made a cross with a snake on it; if the people looked upon the pole with the snake upon being bit, they would live. Some were too proud or had their reasons and would not look and died. That is how sin is; it is real and can lead to disaster if not managed right. Holiness tells us God demands absolute perfection, but we must trust in another since we cannot supply total perfection. Jesus Christ's righteousness is the only righteousness acceptable. That is where holiness comes in. We need to grow into Jesus Christ, becoming increasingly like him. Jesus did the Father's will perfectly. Jesus is the only one in all Heaven and earth who oversaw sin according to God's will in a perfect manner; he did not become corrupt, nor did he stare down his nose at people for not managing it so well. Jesus told the Father, "Not my will, but thy will be done." That is just one lesson holiness teaches us as we follow Jesus Christ as our Lord and Savior. This is what holiness looks like, "Not my will Jesus, but yours be done."

Gerald S Melton

As we identify what is going on, we see: sin sits at our door and follows us around wherever we go. Also, as we make ourselves available to God for his use, Satan attacks us even more. We also take note of the scripture command to resist Satan, and he will flee.

When sin bites, we find ourselves under temptation, stumped, or sinning. Our sin is wrong before God's eyes. We somehow got off the path. We must do a U-turn and run back to God by embracing Jesus Christ. Jesus is the only way to the Father whether we are an unbeliever or a violating Christian. We need Jesus to save us from ourselves.

What has God given us to rely on in the face of temptation? First, God has given us himself. The Father so loved us he sent his Son. The Son offered himself as our sinless sacrifice who took our place on a cross. The Holy Spirit comes alongside us and guides us through our treacherous waters.

Along with God, we have the bible with all the truth inside it. Today, there is all manner of training we could get, even if we are lacking. We also have godly experiences to draw from. With all these tools and weapons, we can be on our way to a beautiful walk with God. We can use these things to address sin. We can follow God's gracious leading in the Holy Spirit. We can repent and enter back into fellowship with God. With resources, we can examine the truth to be ready for the day of temptation. As we enter in, continue, and pursue our walk with God, we can see what is coming down the road and learn how to meet it with God's help and victory. We can learn to plant our steps on solid footing and deal with the sin way before we encounter it. With such a walk with God, we can be accountable and credible to him in word, deed, and our walk.

Again, we talk about the truth in the heart. We must declare our independence from rebellion against God through Jesus's mighty power within us. Let us also affirm God's Word over everything we go through. If that sin has a stronghold, then we must fight it off. An essential principle in warring against temptation is to resist violating others in the process. If we had sinned, ask God to give you a spirit of repentance and exactly how he wants you to repent.

We can deal with sin way ahead of time.

Holiness is essential in dealing with sin before it strikes you. Like an enemy on the battlefield, you must take him out before he takes you out. Sin is just like that: we must deal with sin before wrong has a chance to destroy us. There are specific ways to manage corruption, but the most important is to lay the sin down at the feet of Jesus on the cross and let him remove the evil, the stain, and habit. We must learn not to enter the gates of sin's dominion. If whiskey wets your whistle, do not go down the whiskey aisle in the store. If you have a problem with a bad habit, get help before it destroys you. We need to plan when something is coming towards us. Take precautions to avoid sins encroachments. Finally, pray and seek God as your primary weapon in dealing with temptation. Use your armor as is necessary.

Again, we must discern what part we are in inside the spiritual environment. We must not be deceived about what is going on in that community. Also, we must never make allowance for self-deception. With deception brings disaster for the people involved. We might not perceive a person's demise or a group of people because we allowed a front to take over. Let us be frank about the issues in the community and why they came about. What are they, and what can we do about them? Remember that we should pray these things to God in every circumstance and ask for his insight and help.

Therefore, there must be an underlying truth or value to deal with the sin issue we face. Are we dealing with lust? Then we have options to help us: either we can lay it at the cross, resist, confront the desire, seek the bible admonition "thou shall not commit adultery," or we can pray about it. There is a host of solutions for the specific problem. The best thing to do first is to seek God on the issue, perceive his direction, and go that way prayerfully. Sometimes we must hit the mark by applying biblical admonition. Exercise our salvation over sin and let God strengthen us through obedience to him. As we deal with sin, stay in step with the Spirit, and he will lead us to safe ground. Deal with the evil through biblical admonition; do not

Gerald S Melton

let it get at you at all. You are not sinless, but through the power of the Holy Spirit, you are dealing with it effectively. We must find the underlying cause of the issue, biblically, so we can deal with this sin. Jesus said that we shall know the truth if we hold to his doctrine, and the truth would make us free. We must exercise godliness to obtain the discipline to deal with a particular sin. Evil is living in a state of life without God's influence. So, we, therefore, know that sin's objective is to get us to live in a state without God. What is behind sin? The kingdom of hell is behind sin. If we know our bible, we can begin applying the principles in a book or chapter against the corruption that troubles us. We know by our experience how to deal with it; if not, ask the Holy Spirit's help. Again, deal with all sin issues with credibility and integrity because we are accountable to God.

Acting on truth is essential when dealing with sin ahead of time. God's will must direct our words and behavior. We must know and pursue God's will in our ordeal with sin. We must check our speech and action by aligning those words and actions with biblical and Spirit-directed admonition. If there is a temptation or pressing sin, then rebuke it sternly. One time I had a pressing desire to drink alcohol. I knew that when my family drank, they did not stop with one. There was no moderation with us. So that weekend, I rebuked and fought off the desire, and with God's help, it never returned. Without question, you must resist the sin that easily besets you. The victory is freely given through Jesus Christ's shed blood to the believer but must be enforced with spiritual warfare. We must keep in mind to do things God's way. When we battle sin, it is like fasting, do not let people know you are in the struggle. Unless you need help with sin or want to share about it in a group. I am saying that do not let your battle with sin spill over into other's lives in a negative way. You may need to seek counsel for your problems. Be sure to dialogue about it with God and allow him to hear your pain and desire for his help; do this in faith, and he will respond.

With sin, we must get down to the bottom of it to avoid its consequence. Sin will either cause God to depart from you or you away from God. It is disastrous because it can when left to fester, bring separation from God and death. Listen, when all hell is breaking loose, the knock at the door could be a sin of some sort. Do not open the door and accept any thinking. Accept only that which comes from God. If you leave God out of the equation, you have invited ungodliness right into your heart. That place belongs to God, and he will not share it with others. Keep God in the loop and what his will is over the issue. As soon as we discover God's will, then we must carry it out immediately. Affirm to God his love and will for you and that he only wants the best for you. Let us pray that God's will shall come together and that he will give us joy over it. Be sure to be a spiritual leader in the community we are a part of. Let us be responsible in the community God places us in as a testimony to him. As we participate within our communities, lead, and guide by going through the testing with others to show them how a Christian seeks God and draws strength from him. Do not forget to dawn your armor and fight off the enemy and admonish ourselves according to God's will in the Word. Always thank God for his help and oversight in the process of all these things.

We can overcome sin through Jesus Christ. We do not have to be dominated or a victim of evil with the Holy Spirit's help.

Where has practical holiness gone?

Have you noticed practical holiness is never mentioned anymore? Where are the holiness instructors? When we attempt to live out holiness, we run into real struggles. It seems that we are left to feel our way through the struggle associate with practical holiness. What can we glean from the bible about practical holiness?

> Woe unto them that call evil good, and good evil; that put darkness for light, and light for darkness; that put bitter for sweet, and sweet for bitter! Isaiah 5:20 (KJV)

> And I sought for a man among them, that should make up the hedge, and stand in the gap before me for the

land, that I should not destroy it: but I found none. Ezekiel 22:30 (KJV)

Even after bible school, practical holiness drifts off the scene of understanding, yet the need arises. We find our need for participation in holiness either makes us or breaks us. If we apply ourselves to it, we grow, and if not, we falter. Every setting we are a part of demands holiness if we are Christ's followers. As we apply ourselves in our rural communal areas, larger communities benefit from our candor and trustworthy character.

We either are or live among people who cannot discern holiness or God's call to stand in the gap for God for the land. If we participate in holiness (God's operating in our life), we will discern holiness and how to enforce it. Practical holiness is our cooperation with God in our growth in Jesus Christ. Honestly, people go by opinions instead of bible values. If we cannot discern what holiness is, how can we determine right from wrong? How can we enforce that which is to be kept sacred? It behooves us to learn, apply, and enforce God's divine order. Our battle lies in who we allow to rule us. If we feel our way through, we cannot lead others aright, so our search for answers is needed.

In Ezekiel 22:30 (23-31), we get a description of cursed leaders who lead without God. They lead without God because, in Isaiah 5:20, we see they cannot discern holiness. We honor God by being kept and staying set apart for God's service. We know when we are doing our own thing. We sense God has been put out of our lives through ignorance or indifference to him. This ungodliness is unacceptable.

We are warned of how we cannot escape if we neglect so great a salvation. God desires we seek his face daily for his continued blessing from on high, which is greater than ourselves. The Word of God supplies all we need, but our part is to gather bible truth and prepare by seeking God's help in how we apply ourselves. We may, for example, have a mental illness. We can learn a lot about dealing with it by observing a person in the bible dealing with it. We take our problem along with bible information before God; he can and will favor our diligent desire for his solution and ending. Let us pursue God over all things.

Where is holiness when you need it?

We lack those who can instruct us in holiness. When we discover lack, it debilitates us. Such is how we find ourselves when we are caught lacking practical holiness applications. Practical holiness is a process where we participate with God on any issue in life. We must seek God out, and find his help, and do as he tells us.

> But thou hast fully known my doctrine, manner of life, purpose, faith, longsuffering, charity, patience, persecutions, afflictions, which came unto me at Antioch, at Iconium, at Lystra; what persecutions I endured: but out of *them* all the Lord delivered me. Yea, and all that will live godly in Christ Jesus shall suffer persecution. But evil men and seducers shall wax worse and worse, deceiving, and being deceived. But continue thou in

the things which thou hast learned and hast been assured of, knowing of whom thou hast learned *them*; And that from a child thou hast known the holy scriptures, which can make thee wise unto salvation through faith which is in Christ Jesus. All scripture *is* given by inspiration of God, and *is* profitable for doctrine, for reproof, for correction, for instruction in righteousness: That the man of God may be perfect, thoroughly furnished unto all good works. 2 Timothy 3:10-17 (KJV)

We observe in the above passage that we can be fully equipped for every decent work. That is what scripture can do for us. We will find the most helpful person to guide us through this maze is the Holy Spirit. As we stay in step with him, he teaches us the holiness way. Thank God we are not left alone to figure out what practical holiness is. We discern God's will on an issue and obey him and follow the Holy Spirit's leading in it. How can we get training when the true holiness leaders are exceedingly rare? Holiness must be taught and mentored into our living. Thank God the books of the bible are scripts to live holy lives. If I had not written about this topic, would you have discerned its importance? How could you navigate it? Such is why we must be taught. There are more books on this subject than in prior years, but still too few, but many books lack authority. Many books lack good application of practical holiness to life.

If we accept God's plan, then we must understand and do it. We must know what issues God is addressing for the occasion, and then we must manage it as he tells us through his voice or scripture. We are a lamp on a stand, and our love for God must not die out. If we lose our saltiness, those that get hurt are the world's people, who come under judgment. Our stand is essential but predicated on our relationship to God and his Word. We must use our freedom in holiness to liberate others from bondage. As we encounter the need in righteousness for our participation, let us ask God what our part is in the whole scheme of things.

There is a real struggle in practical holiness.

We must understand a struggle exists in practical holiness. Our task in practical holiness is to identify our battle and why it exists. Is the problem us, sin, warfare, or any number of issues such as testing, obedience, or the like? We must acknowledge our challenge and the steps we must take to overcome any hindrances to cooperation with the Holy Spirit.

In our struggle in practical holiness, we see that if we lack preparation, then we lose our victory. Victory is walking with God and doing his bidding, and by the end of the day, you are still working and walking with God. This kind of victory is vital for any winning attitude. Without preparation, we have no success. Practice is guided by scripture.

> Study to show thyself approved unto God, a workman that needeth not to be ashamed, rightly dividing the word of truth. 2 Timothy 2:15 (KJV)

This verse stresses how we should study to do our preparation. We find that challenges come upon us suddenly. We must obtain the Holy Spirit's direction in our life's calling to achieve success. If we gain friends, we must learn to love and serve others in practical holiness. Training is essential to becoming what God would have us be as we discover his will. We must use our biblical models to grow in a holy way. With God's help, we judge our experiences in life to adjust for his way for us. God is the dominator over our lives, and we must obey God as we enter life's circumstances. God also places us within the authority of secular and spiritual leaders.

In understanding practical holiness, we must know that the struggle to be what God calls us to is real. We must grasp control of what is happening within us and guide our faculties to cooperate with God. Practical holiness sometimes stands for God because some persons may not operate in such thinking, and we must stand and declare God's Word to them. As we contend for whatever reasons, we should not attack others because of mire opinion or because we dislike them for some uncomely reason. Pick your battle carefully and seek God through it. As we go through daily life, we can dialogue with God and expect his communication and direction for us.

We lack structure for building our lives.

We are left to feel our way through life's temptations many times. If we do not grasp practical holiness, then we are left to guess what God expects and how we are to cooperate in his will. Where does our foundation lie? We must prayerfully seek God on how we collaborate with him and why. What is true?

We immediately find ourselves lacking help because there are few competent instructors of practical holiness. Many leaders are ashamed of their shortcomings, so they do not teach practical holiness. But, without those instructions, how can we learn? We see, then, without preachers and teachers who have practical theology training and doctrinal integrity, we will not find the place we need to assess and direct each phase of our lives. We must have some teaching to form a basis to establish holiness as a foundation for our lives. With God and help, we can turn our experience into fellowship with God. It is through trained leaders we learn to say, "Blessed is he who comes in the name of the Lord."

Our experience in practical holiness can change to genuine cooperation with God in the processes of life. We want to move from ignorance to operation in compliance with God's divine will for our lives. It can happen to us. We, as we learn practical holiness, can impact others for Jesus Christ. It is vital that in practical holiness, we serve others in our dealing with them. We must learn to talk to God. I genuinely believe God desires to dialogue with us.

God offers us help for our sin in scripture.

It is important for Christians to avoid "being out there!" We tend to do things on our own and get away from the help of God. Staying in a state of lack and ignorance will put you, "out there." When we recognize that we are "out there," then we need to ask, "God what is the way back to peace, fellowship, and

God's love?" If we will live pleasing to God let us pray and consecrate ourselves to him.

Being dependent on God is clear in scripture. Jesus said he was the way, the truth, and the life, and the only way to the Father. The book of Hebrews expresses:

> And Thou, Lord, in the beginning hast laid the foundation of the earth; and the heavens are the works of thine hands: They shall perish; but thou remainest; and they all shall wax old as doth a garment; And as a vesture shalt thou fold them up, and they shall be changed: but thou art the same, and thy years shall not fail. Hebrews 1:10-12 (KJV)

This verse makes it clear that God through Jesus made all things. Jesus sent the Holy Spirit 2,000 years ago and told us he points to who Jesus is, what he said, and all he did to bring salvation to humankind. We have full salvation and victory as we exercise faith in Jesus Christ. As we study scripture, we become wise to God's salvation. The scriptures teach us to walk with Jesus and that is where victory lies. As we learn bible admonition, we can choose God's leading in dealing with sin. This victory in holiness is given the follower of Jesus as they remain in him alone.

Walking in faith is essential to living pleasing to God and being holy. We, many times, do not know where we are going, but God is taking us somewhere. You should encourage yourself in God as king David did. Be true to God, especially in your heart; so, you can stand against the temptation of the world. Our Goal is to please God and be a witness. This does not mean talking all the time. So, dialogue within yourself to God and know that each man will be judged for his own actions.

From time to time, we must stand for our testimony. Do not do it on your own righteousness but stand on scripture truth. In situations, possibilities arise for our good or bad. If we think wrong and speak wrong, wrong comes to us. We react negatively and unhealthy, so the alternative is to see what is going on and speak the truth to it. We will then gain the healthy responses. When rebuking others, we must know that they are more confused than us. Speak the truth out of love to them.

In talking to situations, speak God's Word to it, and the atmosphere, and any consequence we might be facing. Secretly speak God's Word to people in private prayer time and not using opinions. Speak in your prayer time to your enemies, to yourself; and tell God what you spoke and why.

We must think right and part of this is to speak right things and scripture and faith for God to act.

What does holiness look like?

Holiness needs to be understood. An awe of God is nice, but that does little for our application and cooperation of ourselves in his program. What we end up doing is staying in fear. God expects us to cooperate intelligently with his program for us.

There are three aspects to holiness: 1. We start with instant holiness (positional righteousness), 2. Then we learn to cooperate with God in practical holiness, and 3. We grow into Christlikeness as the Holy Spirit sanctifies us. Let us begin discussing holiness by us being given positional righteousness through faith in Jesus Christ. We learn quickly that we must cooperate with the Holy Spirit in practical holiness or divine cooperation. The Holy Spirit goes on to fashion us into Jesus's image in sanctification. God will use his Word, people, and circumstances to frame our personality, character, and growth into a Christlike person. Our best opportunity to become what Jesus desires for us is to grow in God's meeting houses in the local assemblies, called the local Churches. As we grow and cooperate, God expects that we will model Jesus Christ before a darkened world. The test's this brings is God's chance to reconstruct us.

Positional holiness is where we all begin, and it is given to us by faith in Jesus Christ. Jesus puts us in a righteous standing before God when we believe in him. Then we begin to seek God in divine cooperation called practical holiness. The Holy Spirit keeps working in us in sanctifying us constantly by continuing to make us increasingly like

Jesus. Holiness is essential because it is us staying open to God and his rule in and over our lives. He does the purifying while we cooperate. This is divine cooperation and is likened to Jesus obeying the heavenly Father. Of course, Jesus's obedience was perfect, and ours needs God's help. We learn holiness because without holiness no man shall see God. People either commit to Jesus Christ's Lordship while on their probationary period or they are forced to obey through the fires of hell (where they never recover).

Every day, Satan and God debate who own's you and the discussion is directed according to how you live for God or for self. So, who is your God? We are to grow into the knowledge of Jesus Christ. This requires active participation on our part during our full life span. We live holy or under Jesus's Lordship because apart from his influence is a state of evil; so, we choose to stay in his influential care. Be holy as God is holy. We are set apart to do God's bidding. His work is what we participate in.

We cannot stay ignorant over God's will for us. We must know the gifts God gave us to edify the community that we are a part of. Let us seek God to help us cooperate with him in doing his bidding and do it. We should pray for God to help us live out God's will. God's Word tells us that without God we are just making noise; we must do all things out of reverence for God. The sooner we learn what God's will is, our purpose and what God expects from us; then we can find our place and do God's bidding.

Obtaining instant holiness before God.

Instant holiness is given to the new believer from God. The believer is expected to cooperate with God all his days, just as Daniel continued all his day's serving God and his fellow man. A righteous standing is not self-righteousness. The just shall live by his faith. What is the object of this faith? Jesus Christ and God's promises are the object of faith. The new believer assumes through bad mentoring that they should measure up. Be what God says. But without God's help, that is a fairy tale. God must help. We must get clear that to live out the righteous position we have been given in Jesus, then we must cooperate within the lordship of Jesus Christ and the Holy Spirit.

A righteous standing begins when we enter covenant with God by believing or exercising faith in Jesus Christ and all he has done for us at the cross. It is a biblical principal that at the moment we believed that God justified, saved, and made us his children. Ephesians 1:13, 14. It was by what Jesus did and the Holy Spirit applying Jesus's work in our lives that did this for us. The Holy Spirit enters our hearts, when we call on Jesus to save us, and the Holy Spirit qualifies us by Jesus Christ's righteousness. Our cooperation is to continue to abide with and in Jesus Christ and work with his sovereign hand. Upon being saved we are given sonship and are known as children of God. In these initial stages of God bringing forth, nurturing, feeding, and protecting us; the new believer is vulnerable to assumptions whether true or false. Persons may think either its all-God's work, or it is up to them; but both are unbalanced. These assumptions all mis the mark. A good mentor can clear that up because it is God's salvation which we cooperate by submission to His will. He provides as we exercise faith and obedience in cooperation with God.

In this stage of beginnings teaching the babe in Christ to dialogue with the Word in the inner spirit is necessary. They must learn to speak and think what God decrees for their life, so they believe God. God will call those things that are not as though they were and by faith things change for the better. We also must learn to love and guard our salvation. The new believer should learn, quickly, to talk to God.

Living out divine cooperation or practical holiness.

Divine cooperation or practical holiness is responding to God by faith and obedience. This lifestyle is by choice of will, actions, behavior, lifestyle, motives, and attitudes. Please note in practical holiness we never arrive. We may have a mission which we work on, or even a vision in which we strive for, but we are not the source of our righteousness; Jesus is our source of righteousness. It is through Jesus

Christ we are Christians by his salvation. We choose to continue to follow him by his grace and help. Our actions indicate we are in Jesus Christ and led by him. Therefore, we need the Holy Spirit and must be obedient to him to continue in his leading; so, we can follow his directing voice and influence over us. We need the assistance of the Word of God in such a relationship.

We are responding to the grace and direction that God has provided. Herein is our help: as we pray, meditate, and draw near to God, he pours grace out on us, filling us. We, in response to God's love, cooperate with God by saying, "no," to sin and "yes," to God's will. As we mature in Jesus Christ, we realize our need to know the Holy Spirit and how to apply scripture. The truth of God's Word becomes essential to our way of life. Mentors are wonderful at this stage to help us prepare ourselves. We must learn to practice spiritual disciplines and practice them. The bible will help us progress. God also uses our experience to shape and form our character.

To cooperate, we must train and prepare.

Daily prayer and meditations are essential. We must allow our tongue to be saved. Our testimony depends on bridling our tongue and how deep our Christian language is. Key elements in divine cooperation must be in motion, such things as love, prayer, reading the bible, etc. Talk to God about all things and he will take your life and turn it too extraordinary.

Be sanctified by the Holy Spirit.

> Sanctification is God making us like Jesus by the Holy Spirit. God sets us apart for service and love to God and others. This is God's work and we let him do it in us. God works in us perfecting us into Christlikeness. 1 Peter 1:2, 22.

This whole book talks about practical holiness only, not positional holiness or sanctification. Although this book is about practical holiness, all three aspects of holiness are at work together in all aspects of life.

The power of choice: a privilege and responsibility.

Practical holiness is a choice of either right or wrong. We deal with spiritual forces which tempt us to sin with a power and holiness that is greater than ours. We must realize Jesus already dealt with it; it is already finished. Our victory is Jesus Christ's passion at calvary, which is calvary's power or love.

Continually we are challenged by evil to abandon the ship of faith in Jesus Christ. They tell us that faith is outdated; we have made it past that era. But if you examine the voice of progressive secular humanism, it has not solved any of the issues of the fall since Satan caused it. Every person has sinned because Satan caused the fall; therefore, they are disqualified from eternal life. Only through Jesus and cooperating with him can all people be saved. This is our choice. That choice to be cleansed, renewed, and growing in Jesus Christ is our privilege and responsibility, which is to allow God to work through us to accomplish his will.

Satan, though defeated and sentenced to

the lake of fire by Jesus victory at the cross, refuses to acknowledge Jesus complete triumph over him. While the sentence remains to be carried out after the millennium, we must deal with the opposing forces until God deals with it all. We must wait and do God's bidding until he declares that it is time to judge evil, Satan, demons, unbelievers, sinners, and others. The study of the last things pulls these things together so we can get an understanding of what is going on and so we can be workers on Jesus side.

The power of God to assist us is overwhelmingly present if we choose his help in our living. He has imparted his Word, the Holy Spirit, the Church, friends, and all things to help us. We, thus, dare not neglect the opportunities to move forward with God. Constantly, throughout the bible we are admonished to exercise faith and obedience, to cling to God, hear his Word, etc.

We had better begin to hear and read God's Word because it opens us the right way. We should begin to pray to live out the privilege and responsibility to walk holy with

God, pray out scripture where we are lacking, and give God glory and continue to seek Him.

Choices of right and wrong.

In our yielding to God in life's vastitude of circumstances, we have the privilege and responsibility to choose between right or wrong, and good or bad. As we become aware of the settings of our surroundings and the move of the operations around us; we find we are faced with choices. Our obligation is to make the absolute best choice. How can we make the absolute best choice? We know that if we will strengthen our communities, we must follow the Spirit of God in the community's edification.

We find in that objective our limited power in choice because we are finite beings. We also find that what we do can accomplish much if we are God led. But since we are limited faulty creatures; we sometimes choose wrong and bring negative results. If we want better results, we must learn to choose better. We need basic foundations to make solid choices in the communities we find

Gerald S Melton

ourselves locked into, for the community's own elevation, peace, and equality for all its people. Therefore, our ways (policies) rely on common purpose suitable for the community's reason for being. Each of us need to learn to make choices that allow us to be responsible community participators. Shared governance under authority is a possibility if we understand our choices either follow the divine leading or not. We must learn steps to progress toward the well-being of the people within the community because if the community and its leaders prosper, we all do. Our mission becomes critical and so does the community vision. We quickly learn what works and what does not and therefore what Spirit formed us and His desire to thrive the community: for God's good reason. Whether helping, selling, or profit; we have a purpose to accomplish in community.

We know that the nation that forgets God is turned into hell; and the fool says, "no God." Therefore, our collective and personal choices should be conducted by faith and obedience to achieve the divine results and common purpose, etc. As individuals we must govern our own inner dialogue and make ourselves think and go the right way. When we are assessed, challenged, tempted, etc., we must, by God's help, acquire fortitude to conduct our purpose with leadership. Part of God's will is to do our neighbors right: we alone must obtain courage to accomplish our leadership tasks. We must stay in constant dialogue with God if we will continue to choose the good God would allow us to operate in. We must make place for God to be the orchestrator and administrator of our affairs.

What is going on? Why is it going on? We must ask these key questions while seeking God's help. This is the only way we can find and be able to exercise the ability to work through our crises which attempt to be our obstacle, which if managed correctly becomes our toy, blessing, and pattern of success. Ask, is this how I want to choose to manage this? Is there a better way? Let us look for the healthy response to fulfill our responsibility.

We must face our challenges, first by speaking to it, second by applying ourselves thoughtfully. We must address the situation with analysis and good response. Clean up our messes. We must think about governing patterns in the atmosphere and speak appropriate foundational truths to outweigh and replace them. Seek truth with love and use the law of Christ and do unto others as we would have them do to us. If we will not be truthful to ourselves, we will not escape self-deception or any other type of deception. We need to talk to God over all that is before us.

1. Determine to think right because that becomes the quality of who we are.
2. We quench fear and control our spirit which is better than controlling a city.
3. We use our freedom as an adult so we must use it wisely, helping others, and being an adult in following God.

Dealing with spiritual forces with a power greater than ours.

We must deal with spiritual forces which tempt us to sin with a power and holiness that is greater than our own. We attempt to move forward in God's will for our ministries and get beset. This is when we find demonic spiritual forces against us. We tend to get frustrated, complain, and give up. What we are confronted with is the need for power from God greater than our own. The fact is God has provided that very thing for our success in his will.

It is by God's authoritative power we reckon our spiritual opposition defeated. Scripture gives us plenty of anti-dote and direction for us to begin our forward progress after hitting a demonic wall. We fail mainly because we cannot discern and obey the voice of God's Holy Spirit beckoning us to go the way he directs us. The basic tenants of our faith lay the groundwork for our complete victory. We must spend time with God, aggressively disciple, soul win, and do God's will that we can be fruitful. God wants us to bear fruit. The book of Romans lays the foundation God will have us walk to be fruitful and be in faith in Jesus Christ. As we listen and walk with God, he will point out his presence and victory in us through our experiences. We must not forget to yield to authorities residing above us within our communities.

Therefore, God has given us such power and authority to fight and win against the powers of darkness that is against us. We must do a reconnaissance: get a view of what is going on and how it must yield to Jesus Christ and calvary's power if we want to see it operate before us-suddenly God's power will flow. It is God's will we win while being winsome to others by inviting them to taste of God and make their choice. We must communicate to God in what we are travailing for: people, ministry, God's promises, and commands, etc., while fighting Satan off.

We find that as we face off with evil that Jesus Christ and his finished work at calvary becomes so particularly important for us. As we suddenly are jolted by evil forces contending with us, then we see calvary's victory as our victory in our confrontation. We must sort out wrong thinking such as discouragement, self-ability (the flesh), betrayals, quitting, attacks from fellow believers, etc. We must set all these aside. When those types of ideas reside, we act on faulty presumptions to our hurt. We must see God's truth and stay in step with that. As we contemplate the Holy Spirits help, we can reconstruct how God wants it to be. Let us choose the healthy reply and respond to our crises and trouble before us.

So, we speak the truth over our circumstance in love to people involved. Jesus Christ gave us full victory over sin and all wicked forces. We speak the truth and all God's will into our atmosphere within our communities. Truth with love to people with God's correction is needed. We rebuke Satan's evil scheming above us. We diligently follow God's direction, presence and leading. We obey God and dialogue with him also as a reaffirming of his will.

We guard our way of life and ministry through Jesus Christ, scripture, God's leading and the total victory that all powers must be measured by-calvary's love.

Calvary's power

"I have realized that while it is true, I am not capable of being virtues in my own capabilities, I have the source of genuine spiritual power-The Cross of the Lord Jesus Christ." (Pierce, Ministerial Ethics; page 39).

I believe where a lot of people mess up is when they attempt to put it together or maintain things and ministry by their own strength and resources. When we do this, we are not being holy, but trust in ourselves only. We must spend time acquiring God's favor. We must recognize what is going on and address our independence with repentance and trust in God. We can and should have a measure of independence if we operate in Jesus Christ.

Time in God's presence makes a difference and when we spend time thinking about the cross, it is well worth it. The four Gospels in the bible give graphic description of Jesus's suffering for us. The Holy Spirit points, also, to Jesus Christ's work on men's behalf. He carries on the work for Jesus. So, as we realize, we alone without God, are insufficient in and of ourselves; and Jesus made our way possible by his offering up of himself at calvary. We have complete wholeness potentially available to us; and by the Holy Spirits help God's perfect provision can be realized and acquired.

Have you ever had a battle move upon you, strike at you, and grip you for a long duration? Such battles attack people at various times in their lives. It is particularly important we know calvary's power to disseminate such a battle plus how and when to apply its power. We can resist being a victim just by applying the cross to our wounds.

Jesus told Nicadimus in John 3 that as Moses lifted the serpent on the pole, so that any person could look up; if they were bitten by a serpent and be healed. With our sin, when bitten by it, we look to Jesus' work on the cross and we are healed. That is God's power to deal with all sin in our life. Our part is to keep looking to Jesus and continue to believe and reckon the bite of sin destroyed and negated through Jesus's work at calvary.

Take calvary's power mentally and emotionally and place it on the wound; or take the wound and place it on the cross: where Jesus gave his life and shed his blood to redeem and save us. There is where our wholeness is even if something does not happen right away. We can live for God by this power. We carry-on in truth that such spiritual infirmities were dealt with, which they were!

It is finished!

The power we must deal with when we are exposed to temptation is great: it is the finished work of calvary! "The process whereby the "Old Self," the sinful self-life, is nailed to the cross has already taken place." (Pierce, Ministerial Ethics; page 39). We overlook this power when we are under the gun of temptation.

The next time you come under the influence of temptation, do this: put the force of the temptation into calvary's power. Watch calvary overcome it. That is the power we have neglected to use. Therefore, knowing calvary's power can offset the situation, we should let it be the godly power we use to oversee our temptations. In this way we overcome through calvary's love.

And as Moses lifted the serpent in the wilderness, even so must the son of man be lifted up: That whosoever believeth in him should not perish but have eternal life. John 3:14-15 (KJV)

Jesus told Nicodemus that Moses lifted a serpent to remove the effects of getting bit by snakes. Just so, Jesus had to be lifted on a pole so all who are bitten by sin can look to his work on Calvary on their behalf and live eternally.

If we continually look to Jesus, we can expect that he will effectively deal with the "Bite of sin."

The power of sin: it is an issue with all of us.

Sin is powerful and is an issue with all of us. We each struggle with it. We each have personal stories we can tell. Only we can say "no," to it. Sin's vehicle is temptation, which drives right into our heart.

In a human's world, temptation can arise from anywhere. When it does, we must manage it or it becomes either a failed test

Gerald S Melton

which overthrows us if we do not get a handle on it; or if we pass it, it becomes a thing that strengthens us, a victory. These things arise as an appeal to our hearts and connect to the temporal world. Temptation connects to people beyond our community and if we fail, somehow it is known. We must sow our character one good response to God at a time, so when temptation comes, we habitually sow rightly according to the leading of God's Spirit.

Satan and demons are behind sin and that is the power of it. Anything can be the object sin drives its temptation into one's heart. Materials, anger, depression, discouragement, success, work, or any other thing might be the object behind sin which the gates of hell use to appeal to someone from. It behooves us to understand that sin is a transgression against the one Holy God. Left unsettled, sin will destroy one's soul. It must be dealt with God's way, through Christ's shed blood and repentance toward him.

The fear of the LORD is the beginning of knowledge: but fools despise wisdom and instruction. Proverbs 1:7 (KJV)

Only as we turn to God, admit our sin, and plead for Jesus's help can we gain perspective and ability to put sin away. God must clean and remove it, helping us to do our part. Faith and repentance are the key terms we should know. Often God will let us know we have to deal with a certain sin through our conscience. As we search our theology and Sunday school teachings, we find that we were taught how to deal with it. Now, we must go ahead and deal with the sin.

We are expected to put our sin away. Turn back to God. Pray to God for his help and insight. We cannot do this alone. Pray for total victory over such sin and temptation. Learn to fight and say "no," to temptation. Rebuke Satan. Immediately apply the Word of God. That is our most powerful tool. Prayer, God's Word, and other factors come into play to determine victory over sin.

You may be struggling with sin.

To say we can manage sin and its powerful temptation is an overstatement. We have already suffered defeat after defeat! We need to know that we are defeated without Jesus Christ because we already lost and have little knowledge of the supernatural forces behind sin. So, for our benefit, Jesus went to the cross, so we would have a spiritual birth and a walk with God.

As we encounter sin and strange spirituality, let us ask the Holy Spirit for help. It does not make us less of a person to depend on God. Let us begin going to scripture as our first line of defense. The bible will surprise you with exact answers for today's challenges. From time to time, we will struggle with sin. The Holy Spirit can be a great counselor for us in our time of need. Seek God for his leading through temptation. As we go on in our struggle with sin, remember the basics of faith to help you know how-to walk-through sin and think through it. As you walk with God's help deal with the sin. We must discipline ourselves unto godliness to acquire God's favor over sins dominance. Remember that biblical study helps solidify our resolve to work through sin issues. God will give victorious experiences to back our faithful preparations. If we are stumped, we should seek out authority on the issue from a counselor or pastor.

To deal effectively with sin, we need to see it from God's perspective: we stand in total dependency upon God for how and when to deal with sin. Make yourself deal with it in the biblical and godly way. Enter confrontation to displace sin and remove it. We can only do this by God's grace through Jesus Christ's finished work at calvary. To win our test, we must stand for God's chosen position which we should occupy and win from. Remember to treat others right in the process. Respond to the whole test by dialoguing with God for his help and insight to put sin down.

Remember we are not heroes, but "we are what we are by God's grace." When a temptation hits us, it becomes either a test if we fail it, or a trial we must continue to overcome until God allows our victory to have complete dominance over it. What started our event with this temptation? How did we respond to it? Even if you failed and gave into temptation; it is not too late to change your stand and pick the right route. We could recap if we failed and go ahead to do the right thing. We must apply the biblical solution to the whole thing.

Be in the habit to recognize the temptation, then identify what scripture says about it. Look it up and apply the biblical authority over it. Go on and make the bible the prepared solution. Talk to God and ask his help each step of the way. Make sure to thank God for his help.

My example of temptation.

We all have our moments of temptation; my life is no different. I had a temptation come to me one night which persuaded me to yield to wicked tendencies. My friends what do we do with such attacks? I will attempt to shed light on this area.

I have learned that if we want the victory over our enemy, Satan, then we must resist him. The bible gives unmistakable evidence that there is evil power behind temptation. Evil spirits, evil people, the gates of hell all led by one Satan is behind the demise of man. We had better have established our dependency on the Holy Spirit before the big one hits us. The Holy Spirit, alone, keeps us and leads us through sin. Our training in basic Christianity goes along ways with the Holy Spirits help for us choosing the right way. Our experience plus our good and diligent study are used by the Holy Spirit in critical moments. We must consult God, the scriptures, and mentors for help when we struggle with sin.

As we learn to dialogue during contention within ourselves, God will pour ideas to us that brings victory. The key is to let God work all your spiritual muscles as you prepare in study to oversee your battle. Remember, your inner dialogue is where you set the peace for your soul to dwell on by contacting God and letting him know your allowing him to have the primacy over your life. Wisper to God in your situation and he can come through mightily.

When we recognize temptation and sin way before it comes; we must accept that if we want to be kept by God that we must want to live our lives in accordance with and obediently to his leading. It is our responsibility to seek God out for help. We must identify truth and explore the solutions God puts forth for us in Holy Scripture.

We want to be kept and not jeopardize our position in Jesus Christ or in his Church, so we valiantly fight over the turf we have been given. That turf was not a hand-me-down. It came because God recognized faithfulness in us. So, he gave gifts, now if he gave it then it is ours to steward and guard from the true enemy, Satan.

We are unprepared if we think the gates of hell will not rise in its jealousy and attempt to take our gifts away. We must stand guard and fight while we faithfully steward what God gave us.

Saying "no," to sin.

As we face off with sin and evil, we feel violated and abused; and many times, we are. Our key is to maintain an attitude of continually saying "no," to sin; and to press on without quitting.

This attitude is for your walk and relationship with Jesus, as well as the ministries he has given you to steward. To overcome, we must allow the Holy Spirit to lead us. This is choosing the holiness route instead of the way of battling temptation by willpower. We have a walk and relationship with God to guard. So, we must always walk in readiness of character to put down unsuspecting sinful attacks by the gates of hell. We cannot do this except the power of Jesus Christ's finished work at Calvary is operating in us. We must constantly rely on him to give his full victory over our circumstances, attacks, and temptations.

Our part is to recognize the battle, yield to God, and continually say no to the inception of wicked tendencies. When we become aware of lurking sin then we must deal with it before we come to it. Discern if this is your heart yielding to temptation. If it is, remind yourself that Jesus Christ is your Lord, Savior, and Master. He will direct your heart away or through the evil that is present.

If the temptation is intruding, we put on the armour immediately and strike with our sword. Let the spiritual enemy know God works through you and you are not going to be a victim.

With God's help through calvary's love, we have the power to say no to sin. Our fortitude comes from Jesus Christ as we daily reckon our will to his and let him guide us by his Spirit. He is sitting on High at the Fathers right hand and Jesus is mediating on our behalf. Jesus sends his Angels to help, and he helps us know by his Spirit that he is with us. He is the comforter and helper in our time of need and temptation.

Dealing with temptations.

Temptation may cause us to allow ourselves to be seduced away from God. This bad rejection of the faith could happen by any means or a multi-means situation. If we let go of God, we have been seduced into Satan's trap. Only seeking God pro-actively before Satan has a chance to strike us through with doubt enables us to face off with the proper response. If we refuse to do our preparation through spiritual disciplines and exercising godliness, then we will be caught off guard and will suffer a defeat of not knowing how to stand at that moment for God in the situation.

Again, there are several types of temptations. Some temptations are inner fleshly desires, and others from outside influences. Whether they are inner influences or outer influences, we must deal with them. Deception can come from our own heart or from other hearts. It may not be easy to tell if you are dealing with temptation. So, you must use discernment and manage it correctly. If you manage it God's way, then it has been overseen correctly. Your conscience should bear with you concerning God's will, his leading and his assurance.

Temptation cannot be seen or managed with our hands. We must deal with it in our minds, emotions, and will by the Holy Spirit's leading if we will not suffer a bite from it. The Holy Spirit communicates with our Spirit and lets us know temptation is lurking at our heart's door. The Holy Spirit: 1. Provides a way of escape, 2. Gives us an understanding that there is a right solution, 3. And helps us with the solution whether it is pleasant or hard to deal with.

To overcome, you must analyze where this temptation originated from. Try to pinpoint its origin, then work from there to cut it off.

Consider the source when dealing with temptation.

The source is the identified cause of our temptation, and that source must be considered in how we deal with overseeing the temptation, because we want to cut off the source correctly; or the problem just grows worse. We must also consider the source of our victory and how our connection will bring us victory in every situation.

When is this temptation taking place? If we recognize a pattern, then we are better able to trace the source down. Does this happen at the same place all the time? Does it happen when we do certain things? Analyze were this happens and what takes place. When this happens who is there? Who watches us and comments? What do they tell us? Do we have godly connections? Does God warn us? Do we sin knowingly? What is going on? What ties are part of this? Is it connected to a bigger community then a simple assembly? If so, write out why and all your observations?

We must discover now, why this goes on. Pinpoint in prayer the key reason this is going on. What logic do you have to diagnose this reaction of yours to stimuli causing you to react in a sinful way? Why does it go on, can you change it? You must know its error (to put your finger on it). That way you realize why it is such a real concern to you and God; then you can talk to God about it.

Now tell yourself how scripture speaks to such settings, sources of temptation, and proper responses: you must pray in the victory. What specifics does scripture say? Do a preparation and list main points and the application on it. It is important we align ourselves to respond in faith. Faith pleases God and not a guilty conscience. Now we align to choose, with God's help, how theology touches it all. Write it down and pray it out.

We must take the bible mandate or teaching and apply ourselves prayerfully to it. Pray from day one to forever on getting this right with God. Make sure you know and apply the bible mandates. Plot using some formula to deal with it and for strength and fortitude managing it.

Temptation will bother us from time to time.

When we fall under temptations influence, we have entered wrong spirituality. Many people lack a victorious ability to deal with temptation. A major problem is that people do not share their faults or victories concerning temptation. Something is going on and we know so little about it. We must address temptation with God's help in calvary's power.

As we deal with temptation, we are not to let it grow and overcome us. We must take charge of it, or it will take charge over us. Take charge before sin does! We find an arsenal of equipment at our disposal. Scripture, prayer, following doctrine, study, and training, and more; all the things God gave to help us. We must utilize such information to stop sin. Utilizing our growth to gain additional territory. We must take charge over sin before it takes charge over us.

The truth concerning victory is that Jesus overcame sin at his cross. We must have that firmly in mind because as we move forward with our walk with Jesus, we realize our victory is to remain in him. We need not keep fighting, but we must keep walking in Jesus's victory.

The victory is provided as we walk in it. "We are not in a spiritual crisis and need crises cleansing, but to live a life of overcoming by the finished work of Calvary." (E.L. Biumhofer and C.R. Armstrong; International Dictionary of Pentecostal and Charismatic movements; Page 334).

Temptation will come, but God has provided ways we can deal with it. We must not let temptation get to our head but walk in the victory of Jesus Christ triumph at calvary. We do not have to enter crisis, but we do have to enter Jesus's victory for us through repentance toward God and faith in Jesus Christ.

We each have personal struggles.

Personal struggles come to each of us. What we do with those struggles is determined by many factors: our walk with God, our resolve, our bible knowledge, our obedience, knowing who we are in Jesus Christ, etc. Never-the-less we have personal struggles, so we must know how to deal with the source of temptation when we are victimized by sins lure.

I cannot say that if we are Christians that we are excluded from temptation. In fact, it is the exact opposite. We are saved out of the kingdom of darkness and translated into the light of Jesus Christ; we undergo testing to see our kind of character, as well as attacks from the gates of hell. Remember it was the Holy Spirit who led Jesus into the wilderness to be tempted of Satan. Our beliefs determine the direction of our ministry. If we think we are free from temptation, we short circuit our ministry. If we realize it is part of our probationary period, we will prepare.

It is important to realize we all go through temptation whether we are saved or not saved. So, temptation leads either to failed tests or to victorious endurance in later occurrences. We learn to exercise victory over tests by sowing good one deed at a time in God's directed way.

We also know that people see our struggles and yet will not take responsibility for us, and rightly so. We must, with Gods help, be a spiritual adult and manage our ways with God directing us. Locate where the temptation comes from, isolate, and remove it with God's help, using the flowing blood of Jesus Christ from calvary. Calvary's love will give deliverance.

Be aware that people watch how we manage temptation and know if we are real Christians or not. As we stay focused and locked on to abba Father by Jesus's Spirit, then God will grant victory. Our neighbors watch to verify or vilify our testimony. We must be real Christians in Jesus and we should not give anyone a reason to hate our Jesus. We must be a real role model for Jesus.

Gerald S Melton

Who else is going through this?

Have you gone through temptation and felt all alone? You begin to wonder if anyone else was in your kind of mess. Satan designs encroachment specific to the person. We must declare the biblical fundamental truths to get us out, pray to God, or go to scripture.

We must ask when we go through our crisis and feel all alone: Am I still in Jesus Christ? Am I in crisis cleansing and learning what God is teaching me? Do I need to stand in the finished work of calvary to win this battle? Another thing we must get into our head is this logic: Is my soul hanging in the balance? If you say yes, then you are trusting in yourself and not the finished work of calvary and God. But if you are trusting in God, then your soul is not hanging in the balance.

Now, it is likely your crisis is arising in your failure of faith. God has not failed, and you can trust in him. We must know that our salvation is not hanging in the balance, we must learn that in all situations, circumstances, trials, petty provocations, and crisis's that God has gone through it and goes through it with us.

He will never leave us or forsake us, but he gives confidence for our current spiritual journey wherever we are.

When you are going through a major problem, trust in God. If you are trusting in yourself, then you will fail; but if your confidence (faith) is in God, then you will succeed. Trusting in oneself and our own ability leaves us hanging in the balance of wanting and failure. When we trust ourselves in spiritual matters then we have succumbed to sin. We must trust Jesus and his finished work at Calvary.

As you go through crisis, trust God and his provision by Jesus Christ and his completed work at Calvary which is our total provision now and through-out eternity. Through what Jesus has done, God provides for us eternally. The victory is ours through Jesus Christ, and in fact we already are the victors if we continue to abide in Jesus and his work on our behalf.

The Challenge of being holy
without knowing how.

I do not know about you, but most holiness books seem aloof as if it is something not pertaining to us. Our challenge is to have God's presence and direction abiding with us.

> Trust in the LORD with all thine heart; and lean not unto thine own understanding. In all thy ways acknowledge him, and he shall direct thy paths. Proverbs 3:5-6 (KJV)

> There shall not any man be able to stand before thee all the days of thy life: as I was with Moses, so I will be with thee. I will not fail thee, nor forsake thee. Joshua 1:5 (KJV)

With that said, there remains the question of relevancy: how can people explain holiness at our level in a relevant way? If holiness is the normal sequence in a believer's life; and I believe it should be then who is writing about it in a way, it matters to us? Why is this topic so taboo? Indeed, it is, it is about God's separateness from the created order, and how he calls us to himself, and our reply. But can people help us to enjoin our connect to God in divine cooperation? People lack connection here and little is written on this topic even though there are few out there. Indeed, the whole bible is God's Word about this very thing.

In a since, practical holiness seems to be about God helping us to do our part (obey him) to assure we stay close to Jesus, and conduct his assignment for us, and be obedient in our ministry. So, my plea to the bible theologians is help us to understand this divine cooperation. Give us your personal insights on holiness. The Army prepared me for the gulf war! Who is preparing us to battle sin every day of our lives and that which hinders our walk with God? This is a never-ending struggle. Let us get some teaching so we can win this battle.

Not enough books have been written on practical holiness. How many titles on practical holiness or divine cooperation have you found?

Dealing with daily battles with sin and temptation.

We each must learn to gain insight from God's Word to deal with daily battles with sin and temptation. Whether we like this or not, we must dawn our armour and engage the unseen enemy daily. Ready or not Satan is going to take a case against you. What advice can I give you?

We learn no-matter where we are or whatever community we are in that we will face off in spiritual warfare many times before entering the pearly gates: what can we learn of our daily battles with sin and temptation? We first must stop and tell ourselves that "this is the spiritual norm!" We must proceed to break sin and temptations power off us rendering its influence powerless to affect us. Giving it no dominance over us. We cannot do this any way we want. We must effectively deal with the bite of sin using the shed blood of Jesus to nullify it and render it ineffective. Any place sin and temptation occupy in one's heart must be overthrown.

When we accepted Jesus Christ as our Lord and Savior, sin lost its dominating power. When one accepts Jesus Christ as ones Lord and Savior, the most crucial factor is weighed in the balance: Your salvation is sealed by the Holy Spirit in a process called regeneration.

In whom ye also trusted, after that ye heard the word of truth, the gospel of your salvation: in whom also after that ye believed, ye were sealed with that Holy Spirit of promise, which is the earnest of our inheritance until the redemption of the purchased possession, unto the praise of his glory. Ephesians 1:13-14 (KJV)

From this point on, our responsibility is to walk with God, obey him, grow, and occupy in busy service for him. When we receive the infilling of the Holy Spirit, we become aware of lurking temptation. Satan prowling around looking for a victim. We either yield or resist him.

We must reckon sins tempting power nullified by 1. When we accepted Jesus, we died with him on his cross. We rose with him to new life and victory (not sinlessness) over sins dominating power. 2. We now have the Holy Spirit within to keep us from succumbing to sins dominance. 3. Getting away and spending time with God over sinfulness and all issues of life allows God's favor to move on our behalf.

Where do we go to face off with the ugly corruption of sin? How do we get the power? We begin by asking God to help us, getting alone with God, laying the thing before him, declaring what the bible says; and expressing to God our complete fidelity, faith, confidence in him, and his leading and power to deliver us. Walking with him regularly in such ways while praying and obeying scripture.

Even with all the victories we have ever acquired, it is because the Holy Spirit has kept us. "Always, however, let it be borne in mind that the practical steps we may take in separating ourselves from evil and turning toward God are always a response to the wooing and whispering of a gracious God. Let us also remember that to neglect sanctification is to court disaster." (Menzies and Horton; Bible Doctrine; page 149). We need to also know that even if we sin that God does not give up on us or we would all be toast. He has kept us all by his power.

We can gain power over evil attacks.

As we go through attacks that are evil, we awaken to the realization of an evil force which fights the children of the light. We learn from the bible that Jesus is our power over evil attacks, as we yield to the Holy Spirit, we gain ground. We must stay true to sound teaching and draw from the power of the cross. Finally, we must get in a bible believing Church.

Evil strikes deep into our hearts by challenging our deepest values. Attacks happen when least expecting them, or at high spiritual traffic to shut us down. It is Satan's statement to all surrounding believers in the community settings that he too does bidding in the lives of people. This causes people to question godly patterns and attempt to change the godly ways with ungodly systems. The problem lies in the destruction that comes to communities who have evicted God out, they are turned into hell.

Satan is so subtle such that he stealthily moves in and rips apart his victims. Usually, it is too late after their cry is heard because the damage is done. The attack leaves them sifted. Only the Son of God acknowledged and trusted can heal the sifted ones, like Peter. Satan's goal in sifting is to remove the trust one has in God and his people, so they cannot function within godly community anymore.

Remember the bible's admonition that Satan comes as a roaring lion seeking whom he may devour. We are to resist Satan and he will flee. We must do this resisting within the safe boundaries of Jesus Christ's shed blood and armour. Only Jesus's finished work used by us, and his righteousness put on by us will give the complete edge we need to fight off our Goliaths.

We must jump in our foxhole, dawn our armour, assume our weapon, engage the enemy, fight, and allow our weapons to penetrate. If we do not, God may not be pleased and allow us to undergo suffering, and defeat or continual warfare. We must use his weapons and totally nullify our apposition-Satan or his Goliath who taunts our God. If we spend time in God's presence, we must let our life glorify him in how we fight his enemies.

> Then Moses said unto Aaron, this is it that the LORD spake, saying, I will be sanctified in them that come nigh me, and before all the people I will be glorified. And Aaron held his peace. Leviticus 10:3 (KJV)

There is power over evil attacks.

When we speak of evil attacks we must begin with attitude. Yes, it hurts, and it is unpleasant, but we should not blow up. Rather, we should gain perspective and self-control during an attack. Gaining perspective begins as we ask God to show us what is going on. Gaining control happens long before the day of struggle when we have practiced spiritual disciplines and character.

Observe your crisis and note the spiritual element: how does scripture address it? From that most important biblical viewpoint, pray for the Holy Spirits leading. Bring yourself forward, safely, in the heat of spiritual battle

Gerald S Melton

using a bible model. Romans' steps to progress or Hebrew's declaration of our High Priests superiority. As we step forward unscathed and we possess the ground, we can be sure Satan will take note of our warrior ability and the red sea in the spirit realm will open. If not keep going to the Word and praying for the Holy Spirit's help. When the door does open, ask God to walk you through to His promised land.

Not only must we pass the test of domestic obedience (obedience to God over our responsibilities), but we must also pass the test of inner compliance to God's lordship over us. We must recognize and affirm our love, allegiance, fidelity, consistency, and stewardship to God through commitment to him. We may need to stand or hold a position of sanctifying God before people and in our own hearts. We cannot deeply hold victory if we put God down off the pedestal or our hearts, or demeanor his people by our words and actions. Talk to God as you deal with your inner tests and make yourself think aright toward God, others, and yourself as you have an inner pass and review.

We should ask what was the cause of our conflict? Why did it happen? Did what happen cause us to think or act wrong? Take note. What wrong action did we conduct? Repent of it. Now to change our position and hit the mark of a godly walk, we must ask if our direction from our reaction is where we want to be? If not, where do I want to go? Now respond and direct yourself that way. Ask God for help to achieve it.

Not only are you to obey domestically before God and direct your inner heart to bow to Jesus's lordship (all of which brings freedom and victory); but you must deal with situations, atmosphere, people, enemies, and your own inhibitions by speaking truth with love to them. Speak to each of these things using scripture in truth by love and watch the things change. Last of all acknowledge God, declare his truth, and present yourself in that truth by his love and as for God's good speak it over yourself.

Remember attacks can be so severe that they can maim people for years and even decades. Acknowledge the attack. Realize we must take an attack, contention, threat, or gossip of harm with all sober seriousness. If it comes to your mind, you can be sure someone is thinking of it. If it is thought, then a person(s) might plan and carry it out. That could leave you immobilized. Pray, the Lord rebuke that evil thought against me! Stop it from inception. You must plan your safety out. Not any old way, but God's way. Take note of your attachment to God: 1. Through a born-again relationship in faithfulness. 2. You have been called to purpose and ministry. 3. Your allegiance is to God. 4. You rehearse the tenants of the faith. 5. You pray and read your bible keeping your walk with God up to speed. Stay alive in Jesus Christ!

Yield to the Holy Spirit.

One of the greatest things we can learn in our Christian experience is to know that the Holy Spirit abides with us. To think God is going to make us go through our struggles alone is preposterous. He is with you. Emmanuel (God with us), Jesus is with us in the person of the Holy Spirit.

If ye love me, keep my commandments. And I will pray the Father, and he shall give you another Comforter, that he may abide with you forever; Even the Spirit of truth; whom the world cannot receive, because it seeth him not, neither knoweth him: but ye know him; for he dwelleth with you and shall be in you. John 14:15-17 (KJV)

But the Comforter, which is the Holy Ghost, whom the Father will send in my name, he shall teach you all things, and bring all things to your remembrance, whatsoever I have said unto you. John 14:26 (KJV)

But when the Comforter is come, whom I will send unto you from the Father, even the Spirit of truth, which proceedeth from the Father, he shall testify of me: And ye also shall bear witness, because ye have been with me from the beginning. John 15:26-27 (KJV)

So, the Holy Spirit has come and is with every believer. He imparts Christ's life to us according to John 7:37-39. By the Holy Spirit we are taught spiritual things which gives us the victory. 1 Cor 2:12-16.

It is the Holy Spirit working through his Church who restrains evil. 2 Thess 2:6-8. So, take courage in the struggle you are facing. I understand the pain and problematic situations you might find yourself in being behind the eight ball. But can you find it within you to thank God for your advantageous position in life even if it is so touchy, painful, and ever so perturbed? God is making you, tempering you and you will come out stronger. Keep looking to the Son. John 3:14-18. As you keep looking to the Son with the bite of sin the attack has brought on you, you will find healing as the Holy Spirit applies salvation. He also has sealed you upon you calling Jesus to save you when you heard his gospel. Eph 1:13-14. The bible tells us the Holy Spirit will empower us to serve. Acts 1:8. It is the Holy Spirit who writes Gods law on our hearts. Eze 36:25-29. In this way God enables us to obey him. The Holy Spirit will convict or reprove the world of sin. John 16:7-11. He indwells the believer. 1 Cor 6:19. He sanctifies us. Gal 5:22,23. He empowers us. Acts 1:8. He gives the infilling. Eph 5:18-21. And finally for all advancements, the Holy Spirit gives gifts and offices for service: Rom 12:3-8, 1 Cor 11-14, Eph 4-6.

By the person of the Holy Spirit, we have all we need to be everything God intends for us to be or become. We have no excuse for a wrong attitude. It is our job to adjust this wrong attitude and explore what we are in the Holy Spirit. I adjure you to explore who you can become by the Holy Spirits guidance. The Holy Spirit knows what you do not see, and he puts the right solution in your heart.

Stay true to sound teaching.

We must stay the course in our walk with God. We must use sound biblical thinking to stay this course. If we will prevail over evil attacks using sound teaching from scripture, then we must mentor the unorganized Christian for their own fights against evil. To do that we must use friendships that mentor them through their ordeals. We also should share things which build others up and help them; all from timely Words of life from God and the bible. We use our mentorship to train others to walk the path with the Lord for themselves. We bring God to their need and them to God where they are. We must teach them to maintain where they are so they can hold fast the Christian position in any forthcoming challenge. Younger Christian's need to have basic resources like a bible, dictionary, willingness, discipleship, and a vision to study. We also should teach the Christian offensive and defensive structure to guard their way of life.

As we gain power over evil attacks using sound biblical thinking, we realize Satan roams about seeking a weakness in us where he can devour us. He will attack us if he is allowed by us to do so. Has not the enemy sought to sift you in the past? Has he not sought to make you an object of horror or disgust? You may notice your enemy's strength surpasses yours but compare them to the bigness of your God. Psalms 38:19; 2 Cor 7:5,6; Isaiah 41:13-14 and Eph 6:13-14. We must stir the motivation within to go out and fight in the war for our identity, heritage, culture, family, etc. Eph 6:13-14; 1 Tim 6:12; Jude 3; Mic 7:6; Matt 10:35-36. We must stand, engage, and defend our position of faith to protect our way of life.

We must go to war in God's power and Jesus Christ's victory. Psalms 18:32; Rom 8:37; 2 Cor 2:14. We must be disciplined and persevere, enduring the challenge. 1 Cor 9:24-27; 2 Tim 1:7; 1 Tim 1:18-19; and 2 Tim 2:3. We must determine two things: What source is the attack: Satan, worldly, or flesh. Then we must determine where he attacks: the spirit, soul, carnal nature, the body, temporal, or spiritual life? We are battling against the establishment of some form of influence, thing, or person(s) who are not of God's will. We must use scripture and pray. The gates of hell are trying to manifest. God's Word and his Spirit should be consulted first. We do not deal with all battles the same way but write out our experience and we gain the victory for this same contention the next time.

And when Abram heard that his brother was taken captive, he armed his trained servants, born in his own house, three hundred and eighteen, and pursued them unto Dan. Genesis 14:14 (KJV)

Abraham trained his servants and then pursued the enemy. Before the battle which we might have, we must inquire of God, then go out to battle using God's constructs and advice. Do your work. 1. Know what you are fighting: demons, worldliness, or carnal nature. 2. Where is the attack coming to you? 3. Know your provision for victory-the finished work of Calvary and Jesus's resurrection. God will give you a combo for attack and victory. Eph 6:12 we see we are in a struggle for our freedom spiritually, our culture, our heritage, or our autonomy. We had better take an attitude of defending our own. What does it take to win this fight? We must pay the price for our way of life. We will suffer to keep our way of life. Be willing to sort through the spirituality and obey God by faith, not insulting our own kind of people, though they are different then us. We must live out our beliefs by faith and set our goals. We must determine to think strategic as well as tactical. Securing the spiritual ground is accomplished by the Spirit and an attitude to continue to obey God, while resisting Satan.

Always after enemy battles we must do post battle preparations. Draw out of battle mode to civilian mode when we practice good will again. Permanent peace is the by-product of God's Spirit living within, not any other spirit can produce this peace. Good faith and sound will equal acceptance of one another and helping one another. Good will toward our neighbors' equals being ready to love, help, and serve if called upon in some capacity. We must fulfill God's purpose for us toward our neighbor in good will.

We must consider what happened in our struggle so when it is over, we learn the lessons as to never go through it again. We can refer to the victory God gave us and appeal to the Supreme judge of the earth. We must also do an after-battle analysis and review to learn why we struggled and what was accomplished fighting. If we will keep our victory and precious freedom, we will put those lessons to work. Pray to God over these things.

Warring a good warfare and obtaining the ability to overcome evil attacks takes the use of scripture. We have all been in the situation when we had to overcome in tough storms, or a perfect storm designed to shake us. It could be a battle arising upon us. The goal of such a tool in Satan's hands is to remove the effective testimony of the person. We must guard our ability to defend ourselves with biblical teaching.

We are being attacked because the enemy feels he can attack us without consequences. In Phil 1:30, we see all of us are a part of this engagement we will have. Psalms 140:7, tells us how God will keep us in our day of battle. 1Tim 1:18-19, tells us to war a good warfare. We must remember that Jesus is the captain. Heb 2:10. Scripture resounds with admonition for us to war a good warfare with watchfulness, and earnestness. 1 Cor 16:13; 1 Pet 5:8; Jude 3.

We obtain our victory in Jesus Christ by faith, from God, over that which exalts itself, etc. 1 Jn 5:4-5, 2 Cor 2:14; 2 Cor 10:5. We are to endure the temptation. In 1Tim1:18-19, we must guard our conscience all the time. We must learn to Fight. We must stay in it till it is over. Pray throughout the ordeal and look things up in scripture. Keep seeking God for your way through it.

In our spirituality, we must stay true to sound biblical thinking to win our battles. The true spiritual battles are fought in the mind over which principles are appropriate and how and where God has been leading us as individuals, peoples, and communities.

As you face off with jousting contenders, as you move step by step in accordance with God's will, Word, and leading, you can easily discern which path he is wanting you to abide by.

> Then said Jesus to those Jews which believed on him, if ye continue in my word, then are ye my disciples; indeed, and ye shall know the truth, and the truth shall make you free. John 8:31-32 (KJV)

Our key passage is John 8:31-32. We see

there were some of Jesus own following him; and Jesus's words instruct us as they did his followers:

1. Continue in his Word. 31a.
2. Be his follower or disciple. 31b.
3. Know the truth. 32a.
4. Be free by the truth. 32b.

First, we must continue in God's Word. How do we get to the Father? We get to God the Father through the Son. How do we get to the Son? We get to the Son through the Scriptures whom Jesus said pointed to him. Scriptures can make us wise unto salvation.

Second, we also must become followers of Jesus Christ and his disciples. We can be this type of disciple by a personal born-again relationship with Jesus. A birth of the Spirit. Going on to walk with Jesus. Are we following Jesus and pursuing him? If we know Jesus, then our worldview will be Christ centered and our behavior also. In the assurance of salvation, we will exercise ministry in Jesus's name. We will be a student of Jesus who learns of him and his work cooperating with the Holy Spirit. We will serve others and steward our lives unto Gods will. We will fight the good fight.

Third, we will so grasp truth that we know it and let it govern us and set us free.

Fourth, we will be adults in our freedom serving God and others and using our blessings discretely.

Draw from the power of the cross.

Proper spirituality teaches people to depend on calvary's power when facing off with spiritual attacks of any kind. If you happen to be going through your week and suddenly your spiritually bitten from out of nowhere; you had better be the fighting kind of soldier, God calls us to dawn our armour and fix our confidence on Jesus. The armour is made possible by the shed blood of Jesus Christ who brought us victory through His passion and enabled that passion to be our armour. That armour is symbolic of all the suffering Jesus went through to conquer all enemies.

As you face off with contenders use the blood covering which will reset the whole direction of the temptation of sin off your heart. Study the four gospels which contain the passion biography of Jesus. Studying these passages will enable us to see all Jesus went through. Matt 27; Mark 15; Luke 23; and John 19. Remember Romans 1:16 and 5:1-2. Let these verses convince you anytime sin must be dealt with by the cross of Christ perspective.

Get in a bible believing Church.

We tend to think that just because our walk with God is vibrant that we have arrived. Sad to say if that is your attitude, you are missing a very lot of what God wants to do in you and through you. Part of our Christian experience is the walk; the other part is the public meeting place to celebrate God, meet with him regularly, praise him, hear his Word preached, fellowship and witness Jesus to a lost world.

We must take the time to get or find a bible believing Church: 1. We celebrate God publicly. He gave us our all and he is worthy of public adoration and consultation. God calls us all who follow Jesus to assemble regularly. 2. We are on assignment-we meet with God to get our lives and hearts right with him. He speaks discretely to us in special ways. We must take heed, repent, and obey. 3. We meet to praise our God for all he has done; declaring he is good. 4. God wants to impart his Word to us, so we come alive. 5. God is sending us to a lost, hurting, and abusive world with good news.

The deceptiveness of sin.

The deceptiveness of sin causes the beholder to be unfaithful to God and makes them miss God's will for their life.

Sin if given an inch will take a mile. If we allow our hearts to harbor sin, we will find that we stray farther away from God. Such is the condition of any or all who say no to God and take up a form of sin. Our hearts rarely contemplate the seriousness of the wrongs we do. Because of this neglect in our choice, or having an evil inner eye, sin is allowed to fester and grow and do its damage. Our sin can corrupt our communities, families, ourselves, and our walk with God. We first must know that sin begins with ourselves. Satan is attending the community through us. Satan works through the carnal nature. If we give sway to sins influence; it affects the whole community. We are in trouble for choosing sin over our walk with God.

We can learn what sin is and that is necessary but let us learn what sin does. Two points: 1. Sin causes our unfaithfulness to offend God, 2. Sin nullifies God's will for our lives; it cancels God's will out. We must learn to use the world soberly to accomplish God's directive for our lives. We must keep ourselves in subjection to God and insist that His Word be the authoritative rule over our lives. We all ought to do a study on sin, its dangers, and results. This way we learn how dangerous it is to our life before God. We cannot fulfill our way of life if sin dominates us because a reckoning day will come, and God will require our sin before him.

Sin causes the beholder of it to fall before God. So, we must refer to scripture. Titus 2:12; Roman 6:1-2; Rom 6:14; and Rom 5:1. These versus describe a biblical basis for continued godly dealing with sin. We should prepare ourselves with God's will. We are to nullify sins desire and seek and do God's will that he made plain to us. We must guard our conscience because it is as if wicked spirits can jump onto an unsuspecting person to cause them to yield to sin. Separation: Be set apart for God and his service and live obediently.

> I beseech you therefore, brethren, by the mercies of God, that ye present your bodies a living sacrifice, holy, acceptable unto God, which is your reasonable service. And be not conformed to this world: but be ye transformed by the renewing of your mind, that ye may prove what is that good, and acceptable, and perfect, will of God. Romans 12:1-2 (KJV)

Present yourself to God as living sacrifices. We must learn we have a choice in which we can say no to sin. Sin is that which separates us from God by taking the throne of God in our heart; therefore, we are to say no to sin. Pray to God to help you not to walk in sin or be dominated by it. We cannot do anything without God and prayer helps secure his help.

As one finds himself enmeshed in a Web of sin; they should immediately pray, consult the Word, and repent. Get out of your dungeon. So, pray for God's method of dealing with sin until He gives you victory through it.

Be aware of the deceptiveness of sin.

We hardly know when a sudden and quick attack will come upon us. We also hardly realize when ingrained sin uproots God's will out of our lives. When I was fourteen years old, I was under a pastor in the Assemblies of God. He mentored me and taught me. But I did not realize at such an early age the seriousness of the call or the forces of the gates of hell willing to use any means to corrupt a young person's tender heart or their faith in God. With me, Satan used rock-n-roll music to resist God's good will out of my life. Later when I answered the call to go to Seminary training, I made sure music was controlled and I put out the rock-n-roll. Thank God that he was not done with me yet, as I matured in age the Lord used another group which effectively shared God's Word and drove out all the things hindering his will for my life; all under new and different circumstances.

So, I say that sin (and anything vying for God's place in our hearts) can be so subtle, we do not catch it. We need ears that the Holy Spirit can use to gird us through any seen and known, or unseen and unknown sin. Simply put "if we allow Satan to have one inch in our hearts, he will step over every sacred place to get to his one inch. All the while he will steal, destroy, and trample the sacred within. Because of the seriousness of sin, it will easily overthrow a heart unguarded. We must watch and pray through each temptation. We cannot allow the good deposit of Jesus Christ within to be destroyed and God's plan with it.

For us, it is our duty to watch and guard our heart and spiritual life in Jesus. We have something valuable we must guard before God almighty. If we are unskilled keeping God in our hearts, then the Holy Spirit's seal is neglected; God's salvation is tampered with by our own way of life. We have God's life and holiness within. We must not allow anything to corrupt that.

> And he said That which cometh out of the man, that defileth the man. For from within, out of the heart of men, proceed evil thoughts, adulteries, fornications, murders, Thefts, covetousness, wickedness, deceit, lasciviousness, an evil eye, blasphemy, pride, foolishness: All these evil things come from within, and defile the man. Mark 7:20-23 (KJV)

Realize from this passage it is we ourselves who let the corruption come forth. The only answer I can give is that if you have a root of bitterness; you must calmly wait before God alone and let him have his sovereign way. He alone can help you work through your issue.

We are kept by God's grace.

When we come across that one sinful overbearing time in our life; hear me; God is teaching us a lesson! There will come a time in our walk with God where we just cannot get it right with him. A perfect storm emerges presenting and enforcing sin upon you. This does not happen all the time, but when God allows it. You say in James 1:12-16, that it says God cannot and does not tempt any man. Yes, this is a true, but not always the whole picture. You see God allows tests to come to individuals which determine character, types of ministries, the supernatural nature of their lives, etc. Testing is the only way God, and all the heavenly bidders win their bid.

Let me tell you when sin presses, there is a lesson to be learned. Jesus said, "Apart from me you cannot do a thing." And know without the Holy Spirit, we cannot do a thing.

We get to a place we think we have it down. We think we reached a place we got God figured out. We think we know what he is going to do and what our role will be. We forget God is inscrutable or past finding out. We can apprehend what he allows but will never fully comprehend him now or in eternity. For all of heaven is not an endless series of time, but a continues revealing of the mystery of God from age to age. The earth and heavens; even the highest heavens cannot contain him. God will always continue to delight in revealing himself to his creation, adopted children, and Angels. What is God teaching us when we are overthrown by evil? That, whether we are strong or broken, God is our sufficiency.

There is therefore now no condemnation to them which are in Christ Jesus, who walk not after the flesh, but after the Spirit. For the law of the Spirit of life in Christ Jesus hath made me free from the law of sin and death. For what the law could not do, in that it was weak through the flesh, God sending his own Son in the likeness of sinful flesh, and for sin, condemned sin in the flesh: That the righteousness of the law might be fulfilled in us, who walk not after the flesh, but after the Spirit. Romans 8:1-4 (KJV)

We see in this passage:

1. No condemnation for those in Jesus.
2. For those, though sinners, continue in the Spirit.
3. The Law of the Spirit of life made us free.

4. Our ability in obedience to law and the law is weak, but Jesus overcame and gives us the victory.
5. Though we fail continually, God's righteousness operates in and through us; and through Jesus, sin is defeated.

God is teaching us that being a good Christian is not enough. Being a good old boy fails. Knowing and walking with Jesus is our success. Being covered by his blood and presence is good enough; and should be sought by all. For this reason, God allows overbearing situations. He wants us to know we are what we are by his grace. He has kept us by his grace.

Jesus told us to pray.

Let us revisit the garden of gethsemane together.

> And they came to a place which was named Gethsemane: and he saith to his disciples, sit ye here, while I shall pray. And he taketh with him Peter, James, and John, and began to be sore amazed,

and to be very heavy; And saith unto them, my soul is exceeding sorrowful unto death: tarry ye here, and watch. And he went forward a little, and fell on the ground, and prayed that, if it were possible, the hour might pass from him. And he said, Abba, Father, all things are possible unto thee; take away this cup from me: nevertheless, not what I will, but what thou wilt. And he cometh, and findeth them sleeping, and saith unto Peter, Simon, sleepest thou? couldest not thou watch one hour? Watch ye and pray, lest ye enter into temptation. The spirit truly is ready, but the flesh is weak. And again, he went away, and prayed, and spake the same words. And when he returned, he found them asleep again, (for their eyes were heavy,) neither wist they what to answer him. And he cometh the third time, and saith unto them, Sleep on now, and take your rest: it is enough, the hour is come; behold, the son of man is betrayed into the hands of sinners. Rise up, let us go; lo, he that betrayeth me is at hand. And immediately, while he yet spake, cometh Judas, one of the twelve, and with him a great multitude with swords and staves, from the chief priests and the scribes and the elders. Mark 14:32-43 (KJV)

Jesus was about to be betrayed and his last stop was to pray before his passion began. He attempted to ready his disciples by telling them, "Terry ye here, and watch." Jesus wanted, in the greatest moment of human history; friends praying and watching to see sin and the Master joust. So, they could witness God's victory won through "the unbounded agony Jesus wrestled with in prayer." "Father, all things are possible unto thee; take away this cup from me: nevertheless, not what I will, but thy will.

The greatest victory in history was Jesus yielding himself to the Fathers will, thus, gaining total victory for repentant men. Jesus told the disciples to pray. What might have been the outcome had they victoriously stayed awake, alert, watching, and praying? Would God have granted one or more of them a passion also? We do not know. They did not pray in the victory though, Jesus did. Instead, they entered Jesus' passion in doubt, confusion, instability, and great fear. God could have eliminated all of that. They entered temptation disobediently and unprepared.

Sin is this way. Sin is so deceptive that without prayerful preparation we may not get victory over a battle. Yes, we won the war in Jesus Christ; but winning battles gives us crowns to lay at Jesus's feet. We got to change our attitude. We see in the garden that Jesus was with his disciples (who slept). Yet Jesus battled and won in a lonely desert wilderness experience. He yielded himself to God's will.

Unless we learn to hate sin (have this attitude); that when dealing within, we tell God in prayer, "not my will, Father, let your will be done;" then sin will not be fully dealt with in our lives. We must turn from our will to our Fathers will as Jesus did. As we yield to God, sin is overseen properly and once for all. Let me make it clear that we manage sin through Jesus Christ victory on those prayerful nights.

We must hate sin.

We must not take a "Brush up to sin," mentality or attitude. Sin is rebellion toward God. Evil is living in rebellion toward God. If we will become what God wants for us, we must learn to hate rebellion against God. If we harbor this nature of rebellion or apostasy, then it shows Satan is our father and not God. We must learn to identify the forms of sin and rebellion as the root cause; with Satan being its author. God help us.

We must come to the place where we are bothered, angered, and moved to deal with sin and what it does to us. It severs us from God, fellowship with God and his love and blessings. We must learn to fight for all the goodness God has bestowed upon us or Satan will take it away. When sins influence comes (which is the gates of hell behind it); we must stand our ground and tell Satan "No!" Rise instead of allowing our all to be spoiled by Satan, and fight for the things God has given. Who are we fighting? Not men, nor government; but the power of hell. We go in God's power and not our own. Because sin is so devastating to our cardinal beliefs, we must use truth to counterattack.

What is sin?

English concise dictionary defines sin as "estrangement from God." Sin happens because it is rebellion or apostasy or removing oneself from God and his will for men. It was within the garden where sin was adopted into the hearts of men. God placed Adam and Eve into a garden. A perfect environment with perfection within men and women. A garden with its caretakers. God put a tree in the midst and told our ancestor not to eat. Then, a being in the form of a beautiful serpent came and talked with Eve. He persuaded her to eat the fruit. She hesitated not. The serpent was given dominion over earth in the place of men. God in his long suffering made a way for humanity to overcome the sinister plan of the serpent. God promised a Savior.

> And I will put enmity between thee and
> the woman, and between thy seed and
> her seed; it shall bruise thy head, and

thou shalt bruise his heel. Genesis 3:15 (KJV)

So, sin started in a perfect environment with a lie from Satan to overthrow God's intention for humanity. God had to take his newly formed man and woman through a test to build their character and obedience. Just do not eat of this tree. Satan, though, was jealous of man for having a beautiful reflection of God's image within them. Satan thought of it as a chance to dis-allow God's will for men. Satan still attempts to lead men astray today. So, sin is to disobey God and that separates us from God. Remember, Satan and his demons are the power behind sin. Therefore, we hate sin. Satan is behind it, and it destroys its victim. We must fight it every step of the way.

You must hate sin to prepare.

Sin can cause tough times on all of us. For this reason, we must do preparations to manage it correctly. It was said by my bible schoolteacher that sin is dealt with way before the day we meet it.

We learn in Romans 6:14 that we do not give sin dominion. Either we deal with that thing, or it ruins us. We must take steps to see what we are going through and learn what sin, power, and influence we are struggling with. We must pray to God for proper response. Trust God for the answer and obey him over it. Move on without going back to it. If we need help, get to a paster, or a counselor and get council. Do not let it grow.

We must read our bible. Remember how a man can cleanse his ways.

Wherewithal shall a young man cleanse his way? by taking heed thereto according to thy word. Psalm 119:9 (KJV)

This verse tells us to take heed to God's Word. We must take heed so much so as one walks daily according to God's Word; he grows like a tree by the water. As we continue in scripture, God's Word can make us wise unto salvation by Jesus Christ. 2 Timothy 3:15,

17 tells us we are fully equipped if we study regularly. John 5:39-40 shows us that scripture points us to Jesus Christ and his victory over sin which we are given as our own.

We must listen and stay in step with God's Spirit. He counsels the follower of Jesus in John 14:15-31. The Holy Spirit reveals the things of God in 1 Corinthians 2:9-13. He testifies of Jesus Christ, and we do with him as in John 15:26-27. The Holy Spirit testifies to all Jesus said and did and who he is in John 16:12-14. The Holy Spirit restrains evil through his Church in 2 Thessalonians 2:6-8. The Holy Spirit administers salvation John 3:3, 5-6, 8 and Ephesians 1:13-14.

I can go on and on; you understand that apart from the Holy Spirit, we become nothing.

*We must hate sin so much that
we deal with it effectively.*

Have you ever done something wrong and got so disgusted with yourself that you vowed never to do it again and walked to that end with an abandon? Such is how we must

Gerald S Melton

become toward anything which dares put God off the throne of our heart and replaces him with something else. We must hate sin so much that we deal with it every time it wields its head. We, also, make sure it does not return, so that God has full reign over our lives.

> Submit yourselves therefore to God. Resist the devil, and he will flee from you. James 4:7 (KJV)

This verse is from James a brother and disciple of Jesus Christ. He tells us to resist the devil and he will flee. We must be aware, recognize evil, and sin as it arises. Then give the devil a black eye every time he presents his filth as an option to us. Decide in our mind that we will not let him persuade us. We belong to God, and he will have his way.

> If thou doest well, shalt thou not be accepted? and if thou doest not well, sin lieth at the door. And unto thee shall be his desire, and thou shalt rule over him. Genesis 4:7 (KJV)

This verse warns the person under temptation that sin is at the door. We either deal with sin or it bites us. We must ask God's help, rebuke Satan, and move to do the right thing. Do not bend down and pick up a rattlesnake or you will never forget. You cannot pick up sin, play with it and expect not to be bitten or infected by it. We cannot pretend we have it all together and nothing can go wrong because we are a Christian. We know our strength lies in our being in Jesus Christ. We are what we are by God's grace.

By God's help, it is his will we overcome sins dominance over us (not be sinless).

God's will is that through Jesus Christ's work at Calvary sins dominance over us becomes our victory over it. We do not become sinless; rather we no longer are sins victim because it does not dominate over us anymore. We overcome through Jesus Christs victory. We can, with Gods help say not to sin. Our goal is to be of service to God and one another, edify the community we are a part of.

When we are tested, we either build

character or cave into temptation. We must learn we have a choice according to Romans 6. We can say no to sin, not allowing it to dominate us, and choose God's will in any situation. If we do not exercise character in everyday life by choosing good on each opportunity God gives us; how can we choose good if we are overridden by temptation. The habit of obedience leads us to conquer by God's favor when we face off with evil.

Sin comes to test what manner of person we are as well as the type of ministry we will have. Will we overcome or cave in? We can develop character by dealing with sin as God has instructed.

Plan and prepare to deal with temptations persistence.

Samson was a great man of God. He judged Israel twenty years. But Samson had a problem that led eventually to losing his strength and caused his capture. Samson liked the Philistine women so much that he laid much on the line to be with them. This is called temptation where you lose your gifts and fellowship with God because you chase after something you put as more important than God, his ministry for you, or your life. This is a persistent temptation-a dance with death.

You need a plan to deal with this immediately when you recognize it and to cover yourself with Jesus Christ armour and shed blood. What are some things we can do to help us deal with temptations persistence?

1. Say no! Do not give in.
2. Change the atmosphere by quoting scripture.
3. Immediately pray for the Lords help and the victory.
4. Do something. Get away, flee, and get alone with God.
5. Dawn your armour and fight using anything on hand.
6. Do not sit there and let it tempt you.
7. Get it off your mind immediately.
8. Occupy your mind with something else.
9. Think on the good things.
10. Do not set yourself up for failure.
11. Re-direct your course.

12. If you do not give it the time of day, it will not mind your way.
13. Thank God for delivering you through or out of it.

Know your plan.

We must know our plan ahead of the day of temptation because sin is dealt with way before that day comes. That is a quote from a bible teacher I was under. To deal with this, you must seek scripture admonition and the Holy Spirit's leading.

Many times, finding the passage in the bible which deals with the particular sin we are dealing with helps us overcome it and set ourselves on a godly direction. Doing as the Holy Spirit directs accomplishes this also.

We should go to spiritual leaders and Christian counselors if we need help. Remember though, we got to be the adult and learn God's will and say no to ungodliness.

One more method that may help; try something until you find something that works.

Persevere in dealing with sin.

I want you to know there are spiritual wicked forces behind sin. So, God tells us, "He who endures to the end shall be saved." We are not saving ourselves; we persevere in Jesus's grace. We walk in his salvation all the way to the end.

I believe the doctrine of perseverance to mean we hold to the tenants of the faith as we endure in God's unmerited favor. My experience is that one day I began to lust. The thought would not go away. Then I began to ponder the Cross and what Jesus did for us and how he nailed sin to the cross by his shed blood. I began to contemplate how sin had lost its power at Christ's cross.

> And you, being dead in your sins and the uncircumcision of your flesh, hath he quickened together with him, having forgiven you all trespasses; Blotting out the handwriting of ordinances that was against us, which was contrary to us, and took it out of the way, nailing it to his cross; And having spoiled

principalities and powers, he made a shew of them openly, triumphing over them in it. Colossians 2:13-15 (KJV)

Immediately, the lustful thought left me. That is the power of Christ's cross. It defeated sins power.

What do we do about sins deceptiveness?

Because sin will take you where you do not want to go, and you will end up in a place and condition you do not want to be; you and I must learn to deal with sin or pay a cost. We will fight for our God given victory over it, we will look at how this is accomplished, and we need to know what to do when Satan comes around, we will learn to replace wrong habits, and finally, keep the good deposit invested in us.

Sin can probe its way in anytime and anywhere. We must recognize it and fight to keep our victory. We must learn how we can, through Jesus, keep our victory. As we continue to sit at Jesus feet, we learn God imparts favor for our victory. We, also, hold fast to Jesus when Satan is prowling around like a roaring lion. Let us let Satan know we belong to Jesus and Satan is not our father!

We will learn to take out unhealthy habits and we invest into good godly patterns of success that are biblical. We need to know that what we carry, "Christ in us," which is worth battling for in our way of life.

The Holy Spirit has loved us every day of our lives. We, therefore, have power to love others and God is our ability to be what he calls us to be. We can love because God has put love in us by his Holy Spirit.

Let us be the ones God calls us to be, his adopted children who do his will. We can, by the help of God's Spirit, pray in God's will into people's lives.

Getting the Victory over sins deceptiveness.

We know sin can damage us when left unchecked. We have all been there. The path of redemption is to go to God for help based on Jesus Christ's finished work. We must seek God and his Word for victory. The bible says scripture can make us wise unto salvation.

Jesus said if we hold to his doctrine, we will know the truth and the truth would make us free.

Learn a definition of sin from Random House Dictionary says, "A transgression of divine law." Also, learn what sin does; it cuts us off from God by dethroning him from our hearts. So, sin is an act against God which acts to offend him out of our hearts. Getting the victory is doable by repenting to God and trusting in Jesus to give guidance over sins power. As we turn to God through Jesus Christ, Jesus satisfies God's heart with his sacrifice over our transgression; therefore, God will not remove himself out of our hearts.

The battle with sin is in the heart. We must put sin out or in its place which is under the blood at the cross. Just because we are in a battle, we do not attack people. We love others still. We keep our place during our ordeal by talking to God on what to do and asking guidance.

This is a fight. We must have a change of heart and attitude. We must fight for the value of Jesus Christ's purity within us. War a good warfare by allowing and following the Holy

Spirit on how to deal with it all. Acknowledge God through it all. Observe when sin shows up and immediately apply scripture, set aside wrong thinking, and identify God's will and do that.

Sin, Satan, the world, and the gates of hell makes their appeal to us through the carnal nature through the temporal aspects of our being. We get to guard our person with Jesus's armour and his blood covering. Also, make that old nature submit to the Holy Spirit. Do not, by any means, allow anything to take your victory and steal your walk with God away. Keep your testimony and guard it.

We can accomplish victory over sin.

Wrong spirituality is when we think we must overcome by our power. Right spirituality recognizes Jesus Christ is the victor and we walk in his victory. How do we acquire his victory? We start the day with him and be with him till it is time to sleep, so all day long we walk with him. When we know at the end of the day that Jesus is still with us, that is victory.

Our need is to acquire a new mentality.

And be not conformed to this world: but be ye transformed by the renewing of your mind, that ye may prove what is that good, and acceptable, and perfect, will of God. Romans 12:2 (KJV)

Jesus gives us this mentality as we cultivate our hearts and minds by plowing and planting into the soil of our hearts God's Word. As we do, we are transformed, and we can open to the voice of the Holy Spirit to speak to us because we have practiced hearing his Word and obeying him.

We obtain victory over sin by continuing to believe in Jesus Christ the Son of God. We apply this in all we do as we turn to Jesus by the Holy Spirit in all of life. Sin comes in many forms but is an act against God. Evil is a state in which continues sin has cut one off or separated a person from God. Satan will try to sift persons to enter evil states. We must reaffirm our identity in Jesus Christ and him in us by declaring Jesus Christ is the Son of God. This is proof the Holy Spirit is in us. No man can call Jesus Lord except by the Holy Spirit. And we are in Jesus when we believe.

> But as many as received him, to them gave he power to become the sons of God, even to them that believe on his name: John 1:12 (KJV)

This is how to avoid a state of sifting or losing our identity. We must walk with God and with the Holy Spirit's help affirming Jesus Christ is the Son of God and our Savior. Jesus provided all this in his work at calvary.

This is exactly where Satan attacks, to cut off our testimony. All this is the enemies attempt to nullify our faith. We just must go right on and confess Jesus Christ the Son of God in our testimony. He is good. Through Jesus we have victory over Satan.

What do we do when the gates of hell attack?

The force behind sin is the gates of hell. Satan runs the gates of hell which consists of the fallen Angels and demons. All these are under Satan's influence.

So as demons are like Satan seeking whom

Gerald S Melton

they can devour, we must resist, reject, and strike their every manifestation. We must give the roaring lion a challenging time every time Satan roars his head. To do that we have to learn to put sin in its place. Put sin out of our lives and under God's rebuke. Instead of caving in, submit to Jesus Christ's lordship.

We must learn to deal effectively with sin by yielding to the Holy Spirit and put sin out of our heart and life. Count yourself dead to it by yielding to the Holy Spirit.

Keep confessing and believing in Jesus as the redeemer and lover of your soul. Only because he is the Godman do we have our victory over sin. As God, he atoned for all the world (who-ever believes God through him); and as the Son of man, he was the sinless sacrifice whom Satan had nothing on to accuse him. He is the one we can depend on.

So, fight to keep the good deposit of Jesus in you the hope of glory. Give the devil a black eye and spoil it for him every time he comes around. Do not give to Satan what God gave to you.

Replace unhealthy habits.

You have something valuable to keep before God: your whole person whom Jesus has made full provision for at Calvary. When we get crossed up, we tend to degenerate into consequences of a sinful sorry life. When we recognize that, we should put a stop to it right there! At any time and in any circumstances, we have access to call on God for whatever help and direction we need.

Get out of being dominated by hells gates! Turn to God's sovereign rule through simply turning to him in your distress because he waits to help you.

Recognize where you are. Is it where you want to go? Is it where God wants you? If you are sick of doing wrong, then it is time to repent to God. How do you do this?

1. Call on Jesus for dependent help.
2. Repent where you are at, to God, by being responsive to his help.
3. Stop the bad habit. Do not do that which displeases God.

4. Start doing the right good habits to replace bad ones repented of.
5. Thank God and go on: continue as a new man.

Remember God put a perfect deposit in you.

> To whom God would make known what is the riches of the glory of this mystery among the Gentiles; which is Christ in you, the hope of glory: Colossians 1:27 (KJV)

> Only let your conversation be as it becometh the gospel of Christ: that whether I come and see you, or else be absent, I may hear of your affairs, that ye stand fast in one spirit, with one mind striving together for the faith of the gospel; Philippians 1:27 (KJV)

We learn from the first verse that Jesus within us is our hope for eternity. And in the second verse we learn how to guard that deposit.

1. Your lifestyle should honor Jesus.
2. In all your affairs you stand fast in truth by God's Spirit.
3. In unity fighting the good fight of faith in Jesus's gospel.

This is how we guard our good inner deposit.

Know the good deposit.

As we encounter sins deception, hold fast. Cause yourself to think logically about your God, what he has done for you and how to respond to your spiritual situation. Do not give up your future in Jesus to escape temporary conditions. Do not run!

> And not only so, but we glory in tribulations also: knowing that tribulation worketh patience; and patience, experience; and experience, hope: And hope maketh not ashamed; because the love of God is shed abroad in our hearts by the Holy Ghost which is given unto us. Romans 5:3-5 (KJV)

In these verses we see we are disciplined by the heavenly Father when he proves his love in our lives by pouring his love into our hearts by the Holy Spirit. This love causes us to go through change so we can be conformed by the Holy Spirit to be more like Jesus Christ.

> For whom he did foreknow, he also did predestinate to be conformed to the image of his Son, that he might be the firstborn among many brethren. Romans 8:29 (KJV)

So, we are to cherish the love of God which makes us more like Jesus. That is the good deposit from God.

Do not lay this precious operation by the Holy Spirit on the line. Cherish God's hand in your life and do not refuse God's work within you. Recognize and thank God for his love working in such ways in you.

Remember it's not just Jesus that's part of the good deposit. Many people have labored to secure your position in God. You have prayed to be stabilized in it.

Remember much love and hope was put

into you. That was precious to you. Do not ever throw these away.

How do we find the power to do right when we are tempted?

Have you ever been in a place and found yourself in a vicious cycle of defeat? You could not, for the life of you, do the right thing. Your actions and speech betrayed you. Maybe, you were forced to opt into wrong itself. I want you to know a secret: this is our daily struggle between our carnal nature and our born-again spiritual nature. The battle is within us. We can have a say as we yield to God's Spirit.

I will be suggesting several ways where we can acquire power to go on for God. Usually, at these extremely critical moments in the heat of spiritual struggle, we are confronted with a choice and a result. Satan will put forth a pitch or a challenge to nullify the path of faith and get us to turn to him and away from God. We are confronted with a choice; go to the cross with Christ or deny him and run! How can we say, "not my will father, but thy will be done," if we have not done what Jesus told us to do? He told his disciples to "pray that you fall not into temptation."

If we will not pray for God's help to make the right choices, how will we ever make those choices? Through prayer, we size the opposing aggression of sin before us to God's bigness.

When tempted you need the power to do right.

We have all found ourselves caught in a demanding situation. Where do we, in those circumstances, find God's solitude or find out that our God is a military fighter and genius? God can strategize better than any general ever could.

I want you to know when you find you are under temptation that God is the best war director, planner, advisor, and executioner you can have on your side.

You need to begin:

1. To dig into the vast scriptures detailing God's giftedness in warfare.
2. To realize how God desires to help.

3. To know how to walk daily with God and why.
4. How to approach God for help.

Live life walking with God, pleasing him, and serving others.

To live a life of walking with God, Robert L. Brandt, and Zenas J. Bicket states about Enoch, "While scripture does not state specifically that Enoch prayed, it does indicate a superior relationship with God: "Enoch walked with God." (Gen 5:22). The Hebrew word Halak, here translated "walked," contains the idea of following, adhering to, and so being conversant or communing with God. Enoch's communing was of such proportion that it led to his translation." Robert L. Brandt and Zenas J. Bicket. 1993 The Spirit helps us Pray. Logan Press. (Brandt and Bicket; 1993; page 38).

God's call is to us to walk with him in faith and obedience; this kind of response is what God looks for.

For the eyes of the LORD run to and fro throughout the whole earth, to shew himself strong in the behalf of them whose heart is perfect toward him. Herein thou hast done foolishly: therefore, from henceforth thou shalt have wars. 2 Chronicles 16:9 (KJV)

We are, also, to live a life of pleasing God.

O God, thou art my God; early will I seek thee: my soul thirsteth for thee, my flesh longeth for thee in a dry and thirsty land, where no water is; To see thy power and thy glory, so as I have seen thee in the sanctuary. Because thy lovingkindness is better than life, my lips shall praise thee. Thus, will I bless thee while I live: I will lift up my hands in thy name. My soul shall be satisfied as with marrow and fatness; and my mouth shall praise thee with joyful lips: When I remember thee upon my bed and meditate on thee in the night watches. Because thou hast been my help, therefore in the shadow of thy wings will I rejoice.

My soul followeth hard after thee: thy right hand upholdeth me. But those that seek my soul, to destroy it, shall go into the lower parts of the earth. They shall fall by the sword: they shall be a portion for foxes. But the king shall rejoice in God; everyone that sweareth by him shall glory but the mouth of them that speak lies shall be stopped. Psalm 63:1-11 (KJV)

We must trust and delight in God in good, bad, and always.

We, also, are to live a life of serving others.

Blessed be God, even the Father of our Lord Jesus Christ, the Father of mercies, and the God of all comfort, who comforteth us in all our tribulation, that we may be able to comfort them which are in any trouble, by the comfort wherewith we ourselves are comforted of God. 2 Corinthians 1:3-4 (KJV)

God wants us to serve others just as he has taken great pains to shelter, feed, clothe and save us. We are to serve others in such love and care. This is the power behind that which causes growth. Christ came not to be served, but to serve.

Draw power from Calvary.

We need to learn to draw power from Calvary for our battles.

> Surely, he hath borne our griefs, and carried our sorrows: yet we did esteem him stricken, smitten of God, and afflicted. But he was wounded for our transgressions, he was bruised for our iniquities: the chastisement of our peace was upon him; and with his stripes we are healed. Isaiah 53:4-5 (KJV)

We see four things that grip us in this passage which give us the power to overcome temptation:

1. The good news of what God allowed Jesus to go through in verse 4.
2. Jesus was wounded and bruised which characterizes what he did for us in 5a, b.

3. Jesus' power of Calvary penetrated all forces good and bad; we should let it penetrate our hearts in 5c.
4. We should move on healed, believing in faith in 5d.

We need to regularly review what Jesus went through for us. This simply means study scripture about Jesus' passion. Psalms 22; 1Pet 3:18; Isaiah 53; Gal 3:13; Matt 27; John 19; Mark 15; Luke 23. Continually reading these passages will allow the Holy Spirit to give you a vision of what it cost Jesus to redeem humankind.

Myer Pearlman states, "Through his atoning work Jesus Christ paid the debt we could not pay and secured remission of past sins. No longer does the sinful past hang like a dead weight upon the Christian, for his sins are blotted out, taken away, cancelled. John 1:29; Eph 1:7; Heb 9:22-28; Rev 1:5. He has begun life anew, confident that the sins of the past will never meet him at the judgment. John 5:24. Myer Pearlman 1993, 23rd printing 2004. Knowing the Doctrines of the Bible.

Gospel Publishing House. (Pearlman 1937-2004; page 211).

Choose the right option as the Holy Spirit reveals it.

As we go through life's difficulties, we need to ask God "Lord, please reveal to me the things I need to know by your indwelling Holy Spirit." You will not make the connections that lead to victory without the Holy Spirit. It is important that as the Holy Spirit reveals to you the things going, so that you act on those truths immediately. To fail to do so is an insult to God.

To help you is why the Holy Spirit is revealing things to you.

> Jesus answered and said unto him, if a man love me, he will keep my words: and my Father will love him, and we will come unto him, and make our abode with him. He that loveth me not keepeth not my sayings: and the word which ye hear is not mine, but the Father's which sent me. These things

have I spoken unto you, being yet present with you. But the Comforter, which is the Holy Ghost, whom the Father will send in my name, he shall teach you all things, and bring all things to your remembrance, whatsoever I have said unto you. John 14:23-26 (KJV)

We are those who love Jesus and desire to know God's will that we should obey God in challenging times as well as good times. Jesus tells us if we love him, we will keep his commandments. The Holy Spirit has come to teach us all we need to know to obey God in obedient love.

Seeking to please God is the reason the Holy Spirit has come, so we would have guidance.

I have yet many things to say unto you, but ye cannot bear them now. Howbeit when he, the Spirit of truth, is come, he will guide you into all truth: for he shall not speak of himself; but whatsoever he shall hear, that shall he speak: and he will shew you things to come. He shall glorify me: for he shall receive of mine, and shall shew it unto you. All things that the Father hath are mine: therefore, said I, that he shall take of mine, and shall shew it unto you. John 16:12-15 (KJV)

God still has many things to teach us, and it is the Holy Spirit who will teach us this.

We must weigh the balance
in the right direction.

We are called to stand in the gap for righteousness.

And I sought for a man among them, that should make up the hedge, and stand in the gap before me for the land, that I should not destroy it: but I found none. Ezekiel 22:30 (KJV)

To weigh the balance correctly, we must apply righteousness where it is lacking. When there is vulnerability, we need to build walls of righteousness. We must take time to search what is going on and what God says about it.

By standing in the gap for one's marriage, God's gifts, and even your walk with God; then you will be saving something valuable.

We realize that Satan wants to steal all God has given us. Jesus told us to strengthen what remains and hold fast thy crown. He who endures to the end shall be saved.

Do not throw God's blessings out for sin. Sin is to offend God in some way. Can you imagine that we would wrongly start a cause against our God who has loved and blessed us so abundantly in life? Please deal with the sin before it destroys you.

God can take away what he has given.

And said, Naked came I out of my mother's womb, and naked shall I return thither: the LORD gave, and the LORD hath taken away; blessed be the name of the LORD. Job 1:21 (KJV)

Job was an honest and upright man. God allowed Satan to take Job's blessings away to prove Jobs faith genuine. It would be a catastrophe if we lost all God's blessings because we went off on a rampage of sinning. Do not allow your heart to stray from God.

What do we do in the face of temptation?

> Watch and pray, that ye enter not into temptation: the spirit indeed is willing, but the flesh is weak. Matthew 26:41 (KJV)

We must be ready to pray and then act to sufficiently make it through temptation.

> But every man is tempted, when he is drawn away of his own lust, and enticed. Then when lust hath conceived, it bringeth forth sin: and sin, when it is finished, bringeth forth death. James 1:14-15 (KJV)

We must first realize that the battle starts right in our minds. The moment you are aware of temptation; do not allow yourself to be drawn into it. Temptation conceives in the heart to sin. This is where the whole battle with the giants of temptation oppresses us. It is fought in the mind. Therefore, seeking

God daily helps us be victorious in abiding in God's will.

Secondly, sin conceives and brings forth death. If we do not nip its mental inception, it will work to separate us from God again. Satan and the gates of hell are behind wrong, pushing a wedge between us and God. So, we need to realize who we are in Jesus Christ. We are called out and set apart for God and his service. We are children of God. God make us rulers over the earth and submitters to God.

People goof up on the above fact. They are given over to Satan's way which is resist God and submit to temptation (serve self). They choose whatever makes them feel good or pleases them. They choose self instead of pleasing God.

So let us realize that the battle is taking place in our minds. The choice before us is to either submit to God and have self-control while ruling over our passions; or submit to temptation and violate one's relationship with God. We do have the power to eject thoughts out of our minds and serve God.

(For the weapons of our warfare are not carnal, but mighty through God to the pulling down of strong holds;) Casting down imaginations, and every high thing that exalteth itself against the knowledge of God, and bringing into captivity every thought to the obedience of Christ; 2 Corinthians 10:4-5 (KJV)

We must know how to get the victory over temptation. When we realize we are under temptation, pray for help. Immediately take the right path, do not hesitate, or ponder it. Make yourself think the right way through it. Do it immediately. Make yourself do the right thing. When people procrastinate over doing the right thing, then the gates of hell overthrows their faith.

Get your ideology right when dealing with temptation.

We must get our ideology right when dealing with temptation. What is our theology over what we are dealing with? What do we believe about it? What bible teaching do we have to contend from?

Temptations come in all forms and in all types of settings: you would do well to know what you believe. What are your tools and weapons in your ideological arsenal to help you deal with the many facets of temptation? Preparations are essential for a victorious solution.

Are you being bid on in the heavenly courts? Does your words and behavior match your testimony? Are you bringing your thoughts into captivity? Are you seeking to establish what God forbids? When we realize we have little or no bearing on why things are taking place, sometimes, we need to inquire of the Holy Spirit and do as he tells us to do.

There are many causes behind sin; if we pay attention; we can change things to a godly outcome with God's help. What do you know about the whole situation? Why is this come upon you? This inquiry is for you to learn the 5w's and h about how you can manage this ordeal.

What text and bible doctrine covers the very thing with which you are dealing?

How do you apply yourself in this biblically? How does scripture address it? What is the appropriate passage for it? Is your convictions and conscience telling you anything about the issue? Try to learn what God is saying by asking him in prayer. Cut through the chase and apply scripture doctrine to it.

Does bible teaching address it? We might not be concerned, but if God's Word addresses it, do it that way. We have powerful weapons we can use to help us. Keep applying what you know, and God will help you by his Word. Pray for God's intervention and God will make the difference.

Have a made-up mind to do right.

If we knew a meeting was taking place over us which bid on the type of person, we will become and end our life in an eternal character either good or bad; how would you live out your life?

The fact is in Job 1-2, this wager is being bid on every one of us. God and his angels bid, and Satan and his angels bid. The bid is to determine the conduct, character, eternal destinies and who our true father is (God or Satan). How does that fit in with your salvation and walk? You see, salvation means we have been translated into the family of God and he is our father. Jesus lives in us, and we are guided by the Holy Spirit. What if, within the heavenly bidding going on over us; we keep doing what Satan tells God we will do? What if we reject what God tells us to do? Who wins the bidding then? What we do matters. It shows those to whom we belong.

Can you imagine God and Satan bidding on you? God casts his bid and tells Satan that you are a just man and will not cheat on your wife. Then Satan tells God you belong to him, and you will do it. Then the opportunity arises, and you cheat on your wife. What contempt will that bring to God? Whose fatherhood did you accept and submit to? Who is the lord over you? Whose lordship do you submit to and belong to?

Know and accept this: at every temptation there is a meeting which had taken place over you and bids were waged to discover who you are and whose you belong to. Make up your mind to do God's will. Do not veer from God. Lock on to him and always move to him.

Do your actions and your words
say who your father is?

> Either make the tree good, and his fruit good; or else make the tree corrupt, and his fruit corrupt: for the tree is known by his fruit. Matthew 12:33 (KJV)

Our person is known by our words and actions. Our words and actions speak louder than our confession. How do you make the tree good? The tree must grow up with roots in Jesus according to John 15. We are to build on the solid foundation according to Jesus in the Sermon on the mount. Jesus alone can give a tree excellent quality. But a corrupt tree will produce corrupt fruit. If we receive Jesus Christ as our Savior and give our life to him; the fruit will be good. But a person, no matter how religious, who does their own thing and cares not to walk with God will never have good fruit.

Are you a Christian? You can only be one

by being in a walk with Jesus; a personal relationship of faithfulness to him. There he will make your fruit good. He will make you a tree with good fruit. Give your personality and life to Jesus and he will make you good and right before God.

Two more helps to getting our ideology right.

First, as we discussed earlier, bring every thought into captivity. Again, in practical holiness the battle is fought in the mind. We need to learn to judge inner thoughts and feelings. Are those thoughts of God or not? If not, then eject them. If any thought does not conform to Jesus Christ, then we need to do what we need to do to neutralize it. Replace the ejected thoughts with scripture.

Secondly, do not seek to establish what God has not blessed. God does not want us to go to a bar and start drinking. God does not want us to get into an adulterous relationship because that person belongs to someone else, and we are not married to them. Basically, follow the Holy Spirit. Do not do what you know God does not want you to do;

things clearly set forth in scripture. Reverse this also; do what you know God wants you to do.

We must deal with the underlying cause of sin.

I want to consider three aspects to dealing with the underlying cause of sin. The fact that there are evil spirits behind sin; our responsibility to evaluate the spirits to see what type they are; and why we should never relinquish our authority to unclean spirits.

No-matter where we are and what we may be doing, and no-matter what position we hold; we must be on guard over the influence of sin both from outside and within our hearts. As the prick of sins influence rises, we can be sure underneath is a whole iceberg of power behind it. We must deal with it biblically, firmly, and quickly. We must ask questions to find the underlying cause of what is going on: using the five w's and h, we learn how to deal with certain things especially as we are led by the Holy Spirit, making inquiry of him. As the influence of sin arose, how did it affect or offend others? Did you notice that? It may already be causing divisions and roots of bitterness.

What is the scenario this came up from? What was the cause? Was the influence a contention, immorality, etc. What was its result? By observing the causes and occasions, we can ascertain how it affects the group, community, world, and the systems we use. We need to do our preparations so that we effectively guide the attitude and motive behind the behavior.

We, through prayer and Gods help, can apply biblical truths to drive the wrong from our hearts, community, and atmosphere. What exactly is the bible saying about it? This is the engine to get the situation (heart, community, atmosphere) the way God wants it. We also must pay attention to our conscience, because within our hearts, the conscience will reveal disobedience with which we must deal. Last of all: what is the theological knowledge that tells us how we are to deal with it? Let us look closely and make biblical conclusions and applications.

We must act responsibly dealing with

sin, or Satan will trample our hearts. Pray for God's intervention. When God reveals a solution, then act immediately. Apply the godly solution from scripture. As you work this out, plot it, and apply it; you will see God move in multiple ways which will resolve it, or instruct you on what to do next.

Recall J. Paul Getty who would not forget who he was. We do not want to forget whose we belong to-The Lord God almighty. Ask if the influence and its root sin cause is our reason for being? If not-will excepting it allow me to reach the destination in all good faith? If not-get it out.

Beloved, believe not every spirit, but try the spirits whether they are of God: because many false prophets are gone out into the world. Hereby know ye the Spirit of God: Every spirit that confesseth that Jesus Christ is come in the flesh is of God: And every spirit that confesseth not that Jesus Christ is come in the flesh is not of God: and this is that spirit of antichrist, whereof ye have heard that it should come; and even now already is it in the world. Ye are of God, little children, and have overcome them: because greater is he that is in you, than he that is in the world. They are of the world: therefore, speak they of the world, and the world heareth them. We are of God: he that knoweth God heareth us; he that is not of God heareth not us. Hereby know we the spirit of truth, and the spirit of error. 1 John 4:1-6 (KJV)

Behind sin there is an evil spirit(s) or entity.

Some spirits are aggressive and malevolent. We dare not face off with a malevolent spirit without the help of the Holy Spirit. Apply Jesus Christ shed blood, wear it as your armour. With God's help secured we begin the process of systematically dealing with the forces of evil.

All spirits which are not for Jesus Christ are dangerous and of the devil. We simply apply the 1 Jn 4:1-6 tests to the annoying spirits we must confront, and truth will win over their rebellion.

We are to test the spirits.

The spirit that acknowledges Jesus is the Christ and has come in the flesh is of God. This is how you know. Test, learn, adjust, stand, and move on for God.

Bad spirits are contrary to the Word of God, his lordship, and the work of Jesus Christ. There will come a time you have to confront an entity or spirit which will not cooperate. You use scripture to move it out of the way and secure the ground by the Holy Spirit's help. Prayer is essential in this situation.

Bad spirits are different then the Holy Spirit because they are finite, unholy, and contrary to sound teaching. We need to know good biblical teaching and doctrine to confront and move them out of the way.

Never relinquish your authority to
unclean or familiar spirits.

You keep the Holy Spirit's leading and gifts even if you must fight to the death. God gave you personality, gifts, and authority. Satan would love to hijack you and destroy you. Do not let him. With God's help, confront when necessary.

You must assess the authority and motive of spirits. If they are not of Jesus Christ, his cause, etc., then they are also contrary to you. You must immediately challenge and confront and hit their motive. Shine light on it and they will flee.

We must keep in step with the Holy Spirit and yield to him. The victory over this battle and war is to join with the Holy Spirit and do his bidding. He will not forsake you if you refuse to abandon him.

Confusion maybe an indication of approaching wrongdoing.

> For God is not the author of confusion, but of peace, as in all churches of the saints. 1 Corinthians 14:33 (KJV).

> For where envying and strife is, there is confusion and every evil work. James 3:16 (KJV).

We need to realize confusion is a wicked spirit who secretly pours himself on his victim. The ISBE tells us confusion means shame, wastiness, emptiness, contempt, profanation, shaking, confused, instability, a pouring out together, and others.

1 Cor 14:33 tells us God is not the author of confusion. James 3:16-18 indicates where sin abounds, so does confusion.

> O Lord, to us belongeth confusion of face, to our kings, to our princes, and to our fathers, because we have sinned against thee. Daniel 9:8 (KJV)

Dan 9:8 indicates confusion comes because of sin.

At such times we must rely on the basics of God's Word which we have learned and reason things out godly, biblically, and with the Holy Spirits help. Get alone and begin to pray when you get confused. Psalms 71:1 is a blessing to show us confusion is not God's good will if we whole heartedly seek him.

> In thee, O LORD, do I put my trust: let me never be put to confusion. Psalm 71:1 (KJV)

Tell the Lord, you trust him through what you are going through.

What caused your confusion? Replay what led you up to it. Do this so you can drive it away. What happened that confused you? What did you think? Did you have a wrong reaction to it? Then you must return in your mind to your thinking and response, then change both to a godly thought and response and that will help drive off confusion.

Speak to the confusion truth with love to yourself and others to release that spirit. If it is a detestful attacking spirit, rebuke it with truth.

God is not the author of confusion.

> For God is not the author of confusion, but of peace, as in all churches of the saints. 1 Corinthians 14:33 (KJV)

God never leaves us to be confused about a holy course of action.

> Trust in the LORD with all thine heart; and lean not unto thine own understanding. In all thy ways

acknowledge him, and he shall direct
thy paths. Proverbs 3:5-6 (KJV)

God is in the directing business; he does
not want us to guess what we are to do or
where we are to go. God gives guidance and
sometimes warning.

Evil spirits and sin come in a state
of confusion with no realization of the
consequences of a bad set of actions.

For where envying and strife is, there
is confusion and every evil work. James
3:16 (KJV)

Evil and strife, when allowed to remain,
un-stabilize the people who are given over
to it.

*In times of confusion, we
must seek God's help.*

Get God's directions.

Thou wilt keep him in perfect peace,
whose mind is stayed on thee: because
he trusteth in thee. Isaiah 26:3 (KJV)

As we keep our minds and hearts focused on God, we will operate in perfect peace as he directs our lives.

Seek bible advice.

For all flesh is as grass, and all the glory of man as the flower of grass. The grass withereth, and the flower thereof falleth away: But the word of the Lord endureth forever. And this is the word which by the gospel is preached unto you. 1 Peter 1:24-25 (KJV)

Scripture has Jesus Christ as its object and can guide us through our trouble to God's safe place for us.

Do what you know is right and stick to that.

And that from a child thou hast known the holy scriptures, which are able to make thee wise unto salvation through faith which is in Christ Jesus. 2 Timothy 3:15 (KJV)

Keep going back to scripture repeatedly

and you will always find God waiting there for you.

It's important that we let Jesus and God's things be our pleasure.

Quit deriving pleasure in sin and wrongdoing.

> Delight thyself also in the LORD; and he shall give thee the desires of thine heart. Psalm 37:4 (KJV)

God's desire is to give you the pleasure of your heart as you seek him for it.
Learn to find pleasure in God.

> Fear not, little flock; for it is your Father's good pleasure to give you the kingdom. Luke 12:32 (KJV)

God delights to give us his Kingdom; therefore, make God your pleasure.

Guard your affections.

> Keep thy heart with all diligence; for out of it are the issues of life. Proverbs 4:23 (KJV)

Sin starts in the heart and passions can run wild. Do not let uncontrolled passions take over your heart.

Passions over worldly and sexual issues may exploit your character; so, guard your hearts affections and preserve yourself.

Let Jesus Christ be the object your heart adores. Dethrone the sinful feelings and replace them with scripture affirmations.

If you let Jesus be your hearts delight, God will delight in you, and you will find the path of life.

There is importance to the intrinsic value you have in your heart.

You hold an internal deposit which God and people have invested into you on your journey in life. If you will overcome in your battle over sin, you must know this truth and keep it ever before you. Jesus in you is your hope of glory.

Another juncture in the deposit is how you live out your life. Will you live out your testimony through service to God and others. You must stay motivated and live out your practical holiness by submitting to the Holy Spirit.

Purity must be a priority by allowing Jesus Christ to have a place in your heart without insulting him. We do this by keeping a fresh walk with him.

Your choices are important as you judge whether a course of action is right with God or not. Will your choices negatively or positively affect the important values that keep worth in your heart? We must realize we are carrying something especially important: God's kingdom is in us. Do not defile yourself or put yourself out there. Do not grieve the Holy Spirit in you.

Remember the essential element of God working through you.

We must realize that overcoming is not just making right choices. We must follow the Holy Spirit. This is essential to hear the inner voice of godly direction. This kind of hearing and observing helps us look for the right instructions for our journey. We must be aware of the Word of God and stay in the Word of God.

All the above, helps us observe God's direction for us so we can go that way. Part of this process is to control our inner dialogue. Do not offend God when you dialogue to yourself, nor do we insult ourselves. Be at peace with all involved. Pray for and keep balance. Discern and take the proper course of action.

> But sanctify the Lord God in your hearts: and be ready always to give an answer to every man that asketh you a reason of the hope that is in you with meekness and fear: 1 Peter 3:15 (KJV).

Always persevere in God's grace.

Perseverance is essential. We must avoid the attitude of denying the need for perseverance. Perseverance helps us through each course we walk through in life. We must persevere in any path we are on to come to its end. We are not earning our eternal life, but letting God help us all the way to the end by yielding to God by what Jesus Christ accomplished for us.

The value and purpose in perseverance is obvious after we realize that the Spirit has sovereign right over us. Perseverance, by God's help in us, unto his grace, is valuable for doing any decent work God gives us. Our purpose is to accomplish what God calls us to do.

We must persevere in doing well or God's will. We will all give account and answer "why," we oversaw ourselves as we did. We realize evil is a force against us, attempting to stop God's work in perseverance through us. That same force put Jesus on the cross contrary to themselves. But God used Jesus's cross to bring a future end to the forces of darkness.

We must persevere in our source of power. The gospel, God's Word, and the Holy Spirit are our sources of power, authority, and influence. Let us be clean in these sources and treat them with respect. Remain in our source and grow. Walk in the protection and battle our battles from the sources. Outside the source we become weak.

How do we live a life of overcoming?

Our whole goal is to live an overcoming life. We do this through the finished work of calvary.

What does an overcoming life mean?

An overcoming life means God is in charge and the dominant influence in our life. Also, it means our life is clean through Christ's work at Calvary, the Word of God, and the work of the Holy Spirit. It means we are walking according to God's direction and authority. Thus, we need the bible, God's commands, the Spirits leading, Jesus, the influence of the Church, and the preacher and fellow believers. We also should stay away from whatever would defile us and make us unfit for the person of Christ and his service.

How do we overcome?

We need to listen to what the Spirit says to the Church. We also must stay under the blood of the Lamb. Keep the Word of our testimony. Both are essential when we are fighting battles. Plus, be patient in afflictions. We must endure persecution. We must continue to move forward in faith despite influences against us.

Conclusion

I hope you use practical holiness to help you through the maze of spiritual challenges and temptations that are common to all people in your struggle with sin; so, you can venture out into God's will for your life.

Do not be overwhelmed simply because God is with you and has a purpose for you. He will gladly help you to do his will if you show willingness.

Learning to walk in cooperation with the ways, God set forth, in his Word, helps us to move on and serve God and others, so we all grow in the process.

Apply your efforts to grow near God. If you put off practical holiness, you can further postpone or jeopardize God's will in you. Keep at it!

Look to the cross, there Jesus came to give you full victory and direction to live your life in the Spirit now!

Printed in the United States
by Baker & Taylor Publisher Services